PRAISE FOR KICK-ASS KINDA GIRL

"Kathi Koll's creativity and passion put a buoyant spin on her brilliant caregiving strategies, but mostly I love the way this book places caregiving into the context of life. It isn't about surviving as the child of an alcoholic or as the devoted spouse of someone who's suffered a debilitating stroke; it's about living a life powered by joy, motivated by love, and lifted by hope." —Joni Rodgers, *New York Times* bestselling author of *Bald in the Land of Big Hair*

"Ultimately, Koll comes across as a potential friend, someone who listens well and willingly opens her heart. Since she can't be everywhere to help those who need her hard-won wisdom for moving forward, *Kick-Ass Kinda Girl* is a worthy surrogate." —*BlueInk Review*, a *Booklist* partner

"*Kick-Ass Kinda Girl* is an entertaining roller coaster of a memoir whose second half will be particularly pertinent to caregivers." —*Foreword Clarion Reviews*, 4 stars

"With her husband, Don, facing a debilitating illness, Kathi Koll had a choice to make: She could trudge on, fulfilling her role with her head down and teeth gritted. Or she could choose life for both herself and Don, honoring their time together with joy and energy. In Kathi's new memoir she maps out a plan for caregiving with compassion and hope. Her story is a testament to perseverance, spirit, and character." —Senator Bill Frist, MD, former U.S. Senate Majority Leader, surgeon, and cofounder of Aspire Health

"Kathi Koll's passion and spirit shine. Her story is a stellar example of a life fully lived despite devastating circumstances. Read it, read it again, and gift it to someone who needs a dose of laughter-through-tears along with a lot of inspired practical ideas for caregiving as a dynamic, creative, and uplifting act of love." —Ambassador Nancy G. Brinker, founder of Susan G. Komen and *New York Times* bestselling author of *Promise Me*

"Like the 1984 Olympic U.S. Hockey Team win against Russia, Kathi Koll pulled off a miracle. Her husband Don was not supposed to live for long after suffering a catastrophic stroke, let alone thrive for over six years in the comfort of his own home surrounded by loved ones. I witnessed Kathi's spirited determination firsthand as she actively and lovingly addressed the challenges posed by Don's debilitating illness. For Kathi, *impossible* meant nothing. Her miraculous ability to seize every possibility for hope as she orchestrated with expert precision a medical team that would rival any hospital ICU reveals a woman of great strength and courage. Kathi's moving story is an indelible portrait of one woman facing the impossible with grace and gumption and never giving up."
—Harley R. Liker, MD, CEO of Liker Consulting, and associate clinical professor of medicine at David Geffen School of Medicine, UCLA

"With humor, grace, and raw honesty, Kathi Koll reveals the personal struggles she has faced as a daughter, a sister, and a spouse selflessly caring for loved ones in need. She brings a unique perspective to a universal experience, and her story offers valuable lessons on how caregivers can improve the quality of their lives and by doing so, improve the quality of care they give others." —Donna Benton, PhD, director, USC Family Caregiver Support Center

"In this captivating and touching memoir, Kathi Koll offers a fresh perspective on the relationships that define our families and the care and devotion we give our loved ones. Here is a story of courage, love, and resilience, no matter what life brings. This is a must-read for all healthcare professionals, their patients' families, and anyone in a caregiving role." —Farzad Massoudi, MD, fellow of the American Association of Neurological Surgeons

Kick-Ass Kinda Girl

Dear Dr. Sugarman,
Thank you for
your kindness and wonderful
care towards my husband.
All my best,
Kathi

Kick-Ass Kinda Girl

A Memoir of Life, Love, and Caregiving

Kathi Koll

WP
WARD
Publishing

Published by Ward Publishing
P.O. Box 5470
Newport Beach, CA 92662

Cover design by Zoe Norvell
Cover image © Alita Ong / Stocksy United
Book design and production by Alex Head / Draft Lab

First edition

ISBN: 978-1-7323649-0-5

Printed in the United States of America.

To the many caregivers whose tireless courage and devotion are endless.

The world is a better place because of you and the loving example you set for us all.

*"A single person is missing for you,
and the whole world is empty."*
—Joan Didion

TABLE OF CONTENTS

LETTER TO READERS

If my story inspires anyone, I feel I have accomplished my goal. It's not a how-to, but more of a story of challenges that proves one can still enjoy life and find rainbows.

Why did I write this book? At one time my answer would have been, "I don't know." Throughout my colorful life, friends have said, "You've got to write a book." I'd think of some of my fun experiences, but I always circled around to, "Who'd care?"

Now, I hope people who have found themselves in the complex situation of being a caregiver will find hope in my words. My story is unique, but so are all of your stories. Being a caregiver, no matter what economic stratosphere you come from, is a badge of courage that no one should have to wear. It eats at our hearts and the depths of our being. Caregivers are definitely number two, but in reality they should be number one.

I hope my story helps all of you out there find some kind of a path to follow. My path taught me that today is merely a blink in time. As difficult as it is, life's worth living. In the deepest and saddest moments, somewhere there is a flower just blooming.

I've had many challenging life experiences, and as I look back at them, I wouldn't change any of them. The joy of life is to be able to see the positives no matter how bleak the moments are. Just work through them. I promise you—there really is a rainbow of happiness around each challenge. I've always been rather adventurous, and my life as a caregiver was too. I used to say to myself, "If I can think it, we can do it."

One doesn't need to be trekking across mountains. There are all sorts of adventures. Just the unknown, stepping into an unusual situation and coming out the other end, is the best kind of accomplishment.

It's because of my friend Ambassador Nancy Brinker that I decided to take the plunge and tell my story in a book. I hadn't seen Nancy for a long time, and I'm not quite sure what spurred on my idea to ask her to lunch a couple years after Don passed away. Nancy knew Don while she was married to the late Norman Brinker, the restaurateur responsible for the creation of the salad bar, and throughout the years, Don and I ran into her at all sorts of events and in all sorts of intriguing places. Don always liked Nancy, and we most likely would never have had our special little tie of history if it hadn't been for him. I might have met her, but from the beginning, she's been a part of the tapestry of my "Don Life." We might have been better friends if we had ever lived in the same area or if Don hadn't had his stroke, which caused me to slam on the brakes of many budding friendships. I followed her career from afar—especially intrigued with the fact she was going to be Ambassador to Hungary. Don and I had even hoped to visit her there. Later she was called on to be the Chief of Protocol to President George W. Bush. After Don had his stroke, I wasn't living a life where we'd see one another on a regular basis, but when I did have a little respite and spent a few days in Palm Beach with our mutual friend Tom Quick, I loved catching up with her.

In May of 2014, I was in New York City, and by coincidence, Nancy was there too. I called and asked her if she'd like to meet for lunch. The timing was perfect, and she came with Lynn Sellers, a board member for Nancy's foundation. It was the first time I had seen

Nancy since Don's death, so there were a few tears and some catching up to do on both our parts.

"Kathi, why don't you write a book about your experience with Don," Nancy suggested out of the blue.

"I've thought about it, and people have mentioned it," I answered. "I'm not sure where'd I start, what I'd say, or how'd I go about it."

"I wrote a book about my life with my sister and how I started Susan G. Komen," she replied. "I really think you could reach a lot of people who are going through what you're going through. All you need to do is tell your story just like you've been doing this afternoon. I watched your life with Don after he was ill from a distance and kept up through friends. I have an editor I'd love for you to talk to."

"Hmmm." My mind started racing. "An editor?" I was thinking, thinking, thinking and at the same time listening, listening, listening. The idea was starting to feel a little exciting. Especially coming from Nancy. "OK, I'll call your editor and see what she thinks."

The rest, you could say, is history.

Yes, I've had many sorrows, but most importantly, I've had much joy. I can only hope that in sharing a bit of my story, a piece will resonate with others who are also going through difficulties and see that things can get better.

The circle of life can be such a beautiful thing. Eleven years to the day after Don's stroke, the day that so changed my life, my ninth grandchild was born. I saw an anonymous quote the other day that struck a note deep within me, because it has been so true so many times in my life, "If life can remove someone you never dreamed of losing, it can replace them with someone you never dreamt of having."

PROLOGUE

"You've always had the power, my dear.
You just had to learn for yourself."
—Glinda the Good Witch

My heart was heavy as I made my way through the rolling hills of Connecticut. So many memories of the two Dons who forever changed my life mingled with the weird sensation that I had just been here. Was it because that area never changes? Was it because time seemed to stop, and my last visit felt like it was just yesterday? When my trip began, my brother and my late husband weighed equally on my mind, but as I saw the timeless scenery, the connection to my brother Don became unmistakable. My husband, Don, and I shared many places and memories together, but this quiet spot in the hills of New England undeniably belonged to a love that had been a part of my life far longer.

In so many ways, I'm a seeker of things I don't understand, but at the same time, I'm afraid to ask the questions that might help me find a meaning to the end. I have regretted not asking my brother Don more in-depth questions about his life. He wanted to share, but I was afraid to listen. He had a dimension that is hard to explain and a life enriched with the friendship of so many different types of people.

His unique love affair with the actress Dolores Hart seemed to have the recipe of "happily ever after," but it wasn't meant to be in the traditional sense. She was the love of his life and had always been part of my life from afar. For many years, he struggled through the sadness of his life's direction without her in the traditional sense, but years later, I saw that he came to an understanding that their life was never meant to be as a married couple. I came to this conclusion while watching his interview about Dolores in the HBO special *God is the Bigger Elvis* after Don passed away.

He was so articulate in the interview, which sadly was the last he ever gave. He died unexpectedly shortly thereafter. The last scene shows him saying goodbye to Mother Dolores with a kiss, a promise to phone her, and an uneasy walk down the aisle of the chapel. Dolores had tears in her eyes as she clasped her hands together and pointed them towards the heavens. She told me that those tears were not acting, that she'd had a strong feeling it would be the last time she would ever see him. His imbalance walking out of the chapel in the last scene is difficult for me to watch even now. Don had neuropathy in his feet, an illness Dolores shared with him, and it caused him to stumble from the numbness and pain he felt. It was the cause of the fatal fall he took the following November. One of the saddest days of my life.

My brother met Dolores, an up-and-coming actress who was often labeled as "the next Grace Kelly," when she was in her early twenties. Her long blonde hair and crystal-blue eyes sent men swooning. There was something special, something different about her that set her apart from so many starlets of the day—girls like Paula Prentiss, Yvette Mimieux, Connie Stevens. The story goes that on their first date, my brother fell head-over-heels for her and knew she was the one for him. He asked her to marry him that very night.

Their courtship was true Hollywood in every sense of the word but at the same time very real. They were a young, beautiful couple very much in love. I was in grammar school at the time, so I really didn't recognize the celebrity of it all. Looking at the old movie magazine photos and stories of their courtship now, it looks like a fairy tale. My brother, in his thirties, tall, dark, and handsome. Dolores, breathtakingly beautiful with an innocence that made her even more appealing. Don never had any of these publications on display, but I found them in a box after he died. A treasure chest of memories and years gone by. Many people envied their life together, but the ending was not what most people would ever imagine. It was a true love story of kindred spirits and a personal closeness deep within their souls.

Don Robinson and Dolores Hart

My brother and Dolores included me in many aspects of their life. I was even lucky enough to visit the set of *Where the Boys Are*. The most vivid memory of that day was sitting on the steps of Dolores' trailer when her co-star George Hamilton came up and sat next to me. He said, "Little girl, I've been admiring you all day, what's your name?" I was smart enough at the time to realize that he was just being polite, and his real desire was to get to Dolores. In any event, it was pretty fun for an awkward fifth grader to be "admired" by one of the most handsome young actors of the day. I visited the set of *St. Francis of Assisi,* starring Brad Dillman (so handsome!) and Dolores, where my eyes were opened up to the backstage energy of movie making. I dreamed of being a movie star just like her. She was the first actress to kiss Elvis Presley onscreen. Not a bad legacy to have. A few years later, Elvis called my brother to tell him he wouldn't be able to make his and Dolores' wedding. He really wanted to be there but didn't want to ruin their day with all the hoopla his attendance would bring.

Another vivid memory I have of Dolores was the evening of my piano recital. I was around seven or eight years old. My mom had invited her bridge club friends and their spouses to watch me, but when it came time for me to perform, I was MIA. I refused to get out of the car. I had performed the year before, but for some reason, this year I was scared to death. My mom had me dressed up in the dress I wore as little flower girl in the childhood actress Margaret O'Brien's wedding. It was quite dressy and made out of a beautiful sari fabric from India spun with gold threads. I simply refused to get off the floor of the car. My poor mom was beside herself, especially since her friends were inside the auditorium having to listen to numerous other children playing their piano pieces. Children they didn't even know. My brother asked Dolores to talk to me. She sat on the floor next to me and gently told me of the various times she had had stage fright when she was acting on Broadway. I listened politely to her stories, but in the end, when everyone thought she had succeeded in convincing me to perform, I curtly said, "no." I never left the car, and the bridge club ladies left with my mom feeling so embarrassed that she had put them through such a challenging evening. That was the last piano recital I ever had to be in. Hallelujah!

After a lengthy courtship, my brother and Dolores chose a date for their wedding. Instead of an engagement ring, my brother gave Dolores a necklace with a heart of pearls signifying his love and her name. A few years later, that heart was given to me on my sixteenth birthday, and many years later, I gave it to my daughter, Brooke, on hers. There was a lot of excitement as the wedding neared. We all got together at actor Karl Malden's home; his daughters were to be in the wedding with me, and it was an evening for all of us to meet. The other young girls were Colleen and Ellisa Lanza. Their father was the great tenor Mario Lanza, who was Dolores' uncle on her mother's side. The wedding dress was designed and being made by the famous Hollywood designer Edith Head from lace she had been saving for over twenty years for a special occasion. Imagine how many actresses must have envied Dolores when the news spread that she was the one Edith Head had chosen. The excitement was growing and parties were being thrown when all of a sudden something happened that changed the course of their lives.

According to my brother, Dolores received a letter from the Reverend Mother of the Abbey of Regina Laudis located in Bethlehem, Connecticut, accepting her into their community. She told my brother she had no intention of joining the Abbey, and he was convinced she would never pick it over a life with him. He was confident in his belief but felt Dolores should go there for a couple weeks for a retreat and sort out any feelings of doubt she might have deep down inside. He didn't want her walking down the aisle with any uncertainties and was confident their future life was just around the corner.

"I was on Broadway in the production of *The Pleasure of His Company* with George Peppard the first time I went to the Abbey," Dolores told me. "I had become extremely exhausted from the demands of performances day after day. A dear friend recommended I spend a weekend at the Abbey, but I didn't want to go to a place with nuns. 'It's not like that,' my friend insisted. 'It's a wonderful, peaceful place you can go to for a weekend and come back completely rested and ready for the lights of Broadway again.' At that point, I was ready to try anything, so I spent the weekend. Towards the end of my stay, I felt something inside pulling at me that I really couldn't put my finger on. It was like my inner self was telling me that this place was where I belonged. I felt a peacefulness I had never experienced. I wondered if it might be a calling from God. I shared my feelings with the Reverend Mother who quickly said, 'No, no, Dolores. You're a movie star. Go back to Broadway and be the actress you are.' And it seemed at the time like that was where it would end."

Only a few family members knew Dolores was off to her pre-wedding retreat. Halfway through, she called my brother and said it just wasn't for her, but she would stick out the rest of the time and would be home in a week. The day she arrived home, my brother was at the airport to greet her. The stairs to the plane were rolled up to the door, the door opened, and one by one the passengers descended. Dolores appeared, and when their eyes met he knew immediately things had changed.

They went to dinner, and Dolores broke the news that she needed to call off their engagement. She indeed felt she had a calling from God and had decided to spend the rest of her life in prayer at the Abbey. Dolores told me she had never in her life seen anyone so upset, never seen a man so angry. Don was beside himself. Full of pain and anger and disbelief.

"All of a sudden," she told me, "he stood up. He became very quiet and contemplative. He looked away long enough to compose himself and then quietly took his place next to me. He said, 'If it was another man, I would fight him, but I can't fight God. I want you to know I will love you and support you for the rest of our lives.' And that he did."

For forty-seven years, Don was in contact with Mother Dolores a couple times a week and visited her twice a year until the last visit when their story was filmed by *HBO*. He didn't live to see their faces enlarged on the giant screen of the 84th Academy Awards, where *God is the Bigger Elvis* was nominated for Best Short Subject Documentary. He would have thought it was unbelievable, but secretly, he would have been so excited. My shy brother, who kept their celebrity magazines stored deep in the back of his storage unit. As I watched the award ceremony on TV, my eyes welled up with tears. He had only been gone a few months, and I missed him so much. I was so proud to see him and so wished he was sitting next to me watching. He probably would have been at the ceremony with Mother Dolores. What a photo that would have made. Two young lovers reunited after a life so close yet so far away, walking down the Red Carpet together.

My brother visited the Abbey twice a year and told me that on one of his visits, the Reverend Mother shared with him that the Abbey had been waiting for a time to "test" the seriousness of Dolores' earlier desire to join the Abbey. Mother Superior felt my brother would understand, and that is why they waited to contact her until right before her marriage. It may have been a "true test" for Dolores, but I feel it was a cold, selfish, and unforgivable thing to do to my brother.

Mother Dolores came to Hollywood for the awards. It was only her second visit to Hollywood in the forty-seven years since calling off the wedding. I met her at the Four Seasons Hotel in Beverly Hills. It was the first time we had been together since my brother's death, although we had spoken on the phone quite a few times. She hugged me and asked me to sit down. She wanted to know everything about what had happened to him. Even though we had talked on the phone, it was different being together. It was hard for me to get through the story without crying. She had tears in her eyes, too, but seemed to be able to compose herself better than I.

"How do you do it, stay so calm?" I asked.

"I simply close my eyes and pray to God," she said with the same voice that calmed me in my mother's car so many years ago. I realized it was the same thing she did the last time she was with him while watching him walk away in the tiny chapel of Regina Laudis.

We walked arm in arm to the hotel restaurant where we were escorted to one of the "A" tables. It was strange to be with her dressed in her habit and stared at by so many guests in the lobby and restaurant. A number of people asked her for her autograph and congratulated her for her nomination. It was amazing to witness the number of people who remembered her and were excited to be in her presence. After we were seated, we both had two glasses of wine and giggled and shared stories both happy and sad.

Thinking of that night in February 2012, a faint smile crossed my face as I serpentined through the hills. So many memories of so many people, and here I was, driving to the Abbey all alone. Nervousness chewed at the edges of my attention as I traveled through the winding, forested hills of Connecticut, and within each little clearing was a farmhouse straight out of a Norman Rockwell painting. The sign announcing The Abbey of Regina Laudis popped up as a surprise along the side of the road. It always seemed like such a secret place to me, so I was surprised to see those words displayed at the entrance for all to see. Before turning in, I looked to the left at the small farmhouse I stayed in as a child with the little pond next to it. As a fourth grader, I looked out the upstairs window at that pond, wondering if children ice-skated on it during the winter, because the yellow pollen floating on the top where the stillness of the water never seemed to go away. The pollen was still there. Nothing had changed.

I turned into the driveway, and in front of me was the old red barn attached to the small stone house my brother had stayed in. I felt a tightening in my chest, a lump in my throat. "Please God, don't let me cry," I said aloud. The Abbey was on the right and looked exactly as it always had. There was a beautiful young girl, probably in her late twenties, working in the front garden, dressed in a blue denim habit. Dare I say, "How chic!"? It sounds silly, but I was halfway expecting Julie Andrews to burst open the door singing "The Hills Are Alive with the Sound Of Music."

"Good morning. Where should I go to meet with Mother Dolores?" I asked the young girl.

"Mother *Prioress*," she gently corrected with a circumspect look. Apparently it wasn't unusual for people to show up to the Abbey to try to meet Mother Dolores.

"I'm Kathi—"

"Oh, Kathi." She eased as soon as she heard my name. "Mother Prioress is anxiously awaiting your visit."

I was led into a small room with a grille where the sisters normally met to visit with friends from the outside world. It was the same room where I had visited Mother Dolores years before. The grille had a little door in the center that Mother Dolores opened to squeeze my hand just as she did when I was a child. After a few minutes that seemed like hours, Mother Dolores appeared.

"Let's go for a walk," Mother Dolores said, pointing toward a full-sized door. A moment later, she came through it, arms open wide, waiting to hug me. I felt so close to my brother at that embrace.

She led me through the large wooden gates and into the garden behind the cloistered wall. My favorite book as a child was *The Secret Garden*, and here I was in the Abbey's garden, which as a child, I thought was the Secret Garden I would never see. I had always wondered what it was like beyond the tall wall and old wooden gates. I knew my brother was allowed there, but I never dreamed I would be there one day, too. We walked arm in arm and gently started to explore the years we had missed being in contact. Mother Dolores pointed to the third floor of the Abbey and described what her room was like. She took me into her little office where I met her parrot.

"I always loved birds when I was young," she told me. "I told Don that I heard there was a special parrot in the local pet store, and I wished I could have it. He surprised me with it. His love was completely selfless."

No, his life wasn't as he had dreamed it would be, but I was beginning to see how they had both learned how to keep their love alive in a most unique way. I was beginning to understand what she meant by "Love doesn't always end at the altar." Their love served as a beautiful example later in my life when I had to keep love alive in an unusual situation.

Even after all those years of seeing their lives, it wasn't until this visit to see Mother Dolores that I realized how creatively they stayed connected to one another, how close they were even when it seemed impossible. My brother must have seen that parallel long before I did; he was always so sympathetic towards my challenges and supportive of my dedication to my husband, even as those challenges tested my limits and made life and love difficult. He understood that the connection between my husband and me was deeper and stronger than what a conventional relationship could withstand.

"Head up to the little white guesthouse to get settled. You can meet me in front of the Abbey in an hour for vespers," Mother Dolores said, sending me on my way. I recognized that word through my brother, but really had no idea what it was. I showed up at the appointed time and she walked out with another Sister. Together we hopped into a little car and drove up a hill to the top of the property where the new chapel was standing. I had never seen it before, so Mother Dolores showed me where to go.

"Your brother always chose to sit in that same spot," one of the Sisters commented as I sat down. I could feel him looking over me as I eased in the chair and took in my surroundings. The sisters walked in single file behind the wrought iron grille that separated the altar from the congregation, singing the most glorious music one could possibly imagine. They prayed; they sang.

As the sisters filed out, Mother Dolores fell behind and opened the center gate and waved for me to follow her. I felt the other Sisters were a little startled and wondered why I was behind the altar. When Mother Dolores introduced me, and they heard my name, they immediately chorused, "You're Kathi. We have been praying for you. We all loved your brother so much."

I stayed a couple of days. Not all my questions were answered, but I left with the joy of witnessing a part of life my brother always wanted to share with me.

"Your brother always said you would come," Mother Dolores said into my ear as she hugged me goodbye, "and we would be close one day." I drove away down the narrow driveway, once again glancing at the little red barn that housed my brother so many times throughout the years.

I wasn't gone ten minutes when I received an email from Mother Dolores saying, "I miss you already."

1

THE VISUAL GIRL

"She stood in the storm and when the wind did not blow her way, she adjusted her sails."
—Elizabeth Edwards

My parents were the very picture of 1920s young love. They married after a three-year courtship when my mom was seventeen and my dad twenty. Hard to believe, but in 1928, it wasn't as shocking as it would be today. I never heard anyone speak of my father dating anyone before my mom, and I know for certain he was the only one for her. Their family expanded soon after they were married—with three boys, one after the other. Their firstborn lived only two hours, a terrible tragedy neither of my parents spoke of often. My two brothers that I did get the pleasure of knowing, Arthur—Art to outsiders, but Dink to family—and Don, were born within fourteen months of one another.

They were as different as different could be, but still managed to be thick as thieves throughout their early years, and in some respects, their adult years, too. Brother Dink was the athlete of the family, and when I say athlete, I mean star in everything he did. He was Golden Glove Champ all four years of high school, speed skating champ of California, and a star football player throughout his four years at Loyola High School. A few years ago while visiting Loyola, I spotted a long row of yearbooks neatly categorized by year on a shelf.

I pulled out what I thought were my brothers' years and thumbed through them. There they were. My two stars. Brother Don looking like a movie star, and Brother Art "Dink" the star athlete. I was so proud. Dink was in bold print, full-page photos in every sport, clearly the star athlete of the school. I had heard the stories, but never really paid much attention until those photos jumped out at me. I hadn't even been born yet, which gave me a distant feeling, but at the same time I had a sense of pride that he—Big Man On Campus—was my big brother.

Mom, Kathi, and Dad

I came along much later. My mom never called me a "mistake," although I clearly was. She always said, "We prayed for years to have a little girl." The fact that my brothers were nineteen and twenty years older than I often leads people to believe we weren't very close, but we were. With Don, it came naturally; we were always like two peas in a pod. Dink was a different story. He was tough on me, and as a young girl I sometimes felt he just didn't like me. If he were here today, he'd probably argue this point with me, but sometimes I really felt I just couldn't do anything right for him. Our story was a difficult one of sibling rivalry, or maybe it was just a strain from our dramatic age difference. Looking back, it might have been unrecognized jealousy toward my relationship with Don, or jealousy of the advantages I received since my parents were older and more established by the time I came along. Maybe it was just the simple fact that I was a different generation, and he didn't have time to deal with me. Whatever the case may be, it caused me great heartache, but the tough times in life are building blocks for our character, and he was tremendously influential in helping me become the woman I am today. I'll never know his side of the story, though. He never had the opportunity to see me grow into a mature young woman or the adult who I hoped he would have embraced and been proud of.

Dink married when I was still a toddler, so he was forging a new track beyond life with my parents and me. Soon after their wedding, Dink and Barbara—his high school sweetheart-turned-blushing bride—were on their way to basic training for the US Air Force. Since he was a member of ROTC in college, Dink started as a commissioned officer in a career he believed would be his lifelong profession.

There's just something special about an Air Force pilot. Not sure if my initial impression started because of the movie *Top Gun*, but all I know is whether a guy is a pilot in the Air Force or Navy, he's something special. A breed unto itself. Tough, sexy, strong—real men, not boys. Don, the man who later became my husband, was in the Air Force at the same time as Dink, and it was a time of growth, maturity, and difficulty. It's a life that is hard to understand unless one has experienced it. I loved hearing my brother's, and later my husband

Don's, stories, and I know those days were some of the happiest of both their lives.

When I entered third grade, my parents decided to have me switch schools for reasons I will never fathom. I was happy at Notre Dame Academy, and it was close enough to my house that I could even walk. A journey that most young parents today would never allow their second graders to do in a large metropolitan city like Los Angeles.

My walk wasn't far, but there was a little grocery store and gas station on the way where I bought a few pieces of candy almost daily to make my walk a "treat." I didn't want to leave my best friend, my partner in crime, who I constantly got into trouble with for talking too much. As punishment, we had to write one hundred sentences every day during recess on the steps of the school, shortening our playtime considerably.

Most likely, my brother Don persuaded my parents to switch schools since many of the girls he dated in high school were from Marymount, and my parents always thought were lovely young women with confidence and style. We were also about to move, and my new school was closer to my new house, although my solo walking days would be over.

On a typical warm California day in September, I walked into my new school with my mom. I didn't know anyone—not one single kid—and it's the first time I remember having butterflies in my stomach. What was this strange place with nuns who wore habits that not only covered their entire bodies but most of their faces, too? Notre Dame had nuns, but I could see more of their faces. My mom held my hand as we walked down the mirror-like, polished corridor to my new classroom. I was wearing my new blue-and-white saddle shoes, navy blue jumper trimmed with scallops, and a crisp puffed-sleeved blouse with a Peter Pan collar covered by a navy blazer trimmed with white piping. Topping it off was my blue beret, cocked to one side so my ponytail, tied with a white grosgrain ribbon, peeked out.

"Mommy," I asked as we walked past girls doing a strange plié I'd never seen, "what are they doing?"

"They're curtsying," she answered with a smile. "It's a sign of respect to adults."

Wow, I thought. *Will I have to do that?* I was used to running down the hill from our home and watching the trains go by, hiking the dirt path to the house behind ours, playing in mud after it rained, climbing the large sycamore trees framing my house. I was a tomboy. My new surroundings felt so strange. On top of the uniforms and curtsies, there were no boys. I'd never been to an all-girls school. What were my parents getting me into?

As I quietly took my spot at my new desk, I could feel the other girls looking at me. They weren't being mean; they were just curious about the new girl. When the recess bell rang, the class rose in unison and lined up at the classroom door anxiously waiting to get out onto the schoolyard. I followed suit with a little lump in my throat. I wanted my friends back. I stood alone in the play yard. *Don't these kids know I'm fun?* Across the yard, I noticed a girl walking my way.

"Hi, I'm Lucie. Do you want to be my friend?" she asked.

"Sure," I said.

"OK," she said, taking my hand. "Let's go play."

Even as a child, there's something comforting about a person holding your hand. Here was a little girl who didn't have to help or take care of me, but she welcomed me into this wholly new place without a single reservation. Her generosity of spirit eased my nerves that day and many days.

I wasn't aware at the time that Lucie was the daughter of Lucille Ball. It wouldn't have mattered, but once I found out, I thought it must be so exciting to have a "funny" mother. *I Love Lucy* was my favorite TV show. I imagined Lucie's kitchen with a conveyor belt for her mom to wrap chocolates, or was that how she made Lucie's lunches? Was there a large wooden vat in her backyard for her mom to squish grapes with her feet? Whose mom did these kinds of things? I thought she was so lucky. Did her dad sing "Babalu" every night? What was her brother Little Ricky like? Reality and TV were one and the same for me then, but soon I learned it was make-believe. Her mom was actually quite serious. Ethel and Fred weren't her real neighbors, and her brother's name was Little Desi, not Little Ricky.

Lucie became my best friend.

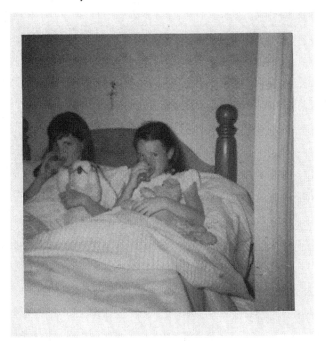

Kathi and Lucie Arnaz

"Do you want to come over to my house and spend the night?" I asked her. "I have an extra bike and fun trails that lead down to a canyon behind my house." We couldn't wait for the day to arrive. I found out later it was Lucie's first overnight.

"Kathi," my mom said, "go outside and wait for Lucie. She'll be here any minute." My house was at the end of a cul-de-sac with only a few homes on it. I always loved the curved red-brick walkway that led to our front door. It was lined with little rose trees my dad had planted. As I rode my bike back and forth on the sidewalk, I wondered why all the neighbors were in their front yards. One man was mowing his grass, another lady cutting flowers, another standing in her driveway reading her mail. Even my dad was home from work, which was unusual for that time of day.

In the distance, the nose of a black car peeked over the hill. It was the biggest car I had ever seen—the first limousine I had ever seen. It slowly made its way past the staring neighbors, who by now were frozen in place, hypnotized by the car.

The limo drove right into my driveway and out jumped little Lucie. Slowly a woman with red hair followed. It was Lucie's mother. I looked toward my front door, and there was my mom in her very favorite dress. It finally dawned on me what was going on: The real *I Love Lucy* was at our house. It was probably the biggest thing that had ever happened on our little street. Maybe it's because I was young, or maybe she was just really that hard to impress, but I had never seen my mother look at anyone the way she beamed at Lucille Ball as she made her way up our path. I hoped that one day she would look at me and my life with that same pride and awe.

My mom invited Lucy into the living room, where they sat down getting to know one another. Since it was Lucie's first sleepover, I guess her mom wanted to meet my family and make sure we were alright. Before you knew it, Lucy and my mom were sitting side by side on the piano bench playing a duet. Lucie and I groaned, wondering when all the fuss would be over. We just wanted to go outside and play.

As our friendship bloomed, we spent plenty of beautiful Southern California days taking in the sun while riding bikes and hiking at my house, and putting on little plays at her home in Beverly Hills. Even though there was no lunch-making conveyor belt or wooden vat for grape squishing, that didn't mean that Lucie wasn't the star of our friendship. She was always the lead in our makeshift plays while I was a maid or gardener or other lesser character. I never questioned it, though, because it was her house, her garage, her stage. She was the undeniable tip-top of the pecking order, but seeing that self-assurance helped me identify it in myself and foster it. Having Lucie as a friend taught me a lot about the difference between outsiders' perceptions and reality, which has turned out to be a common thread throughout my life.

Complicated relationships were par for the course in my family. There was always more than met the eye. My dad was a very kind and calming personality in my life. My mom was the fiery Irish one. The one huge problem—the only problem with my dad, as far as I could see—was his drinking. It was a constant issue during my parents' entire marriage and the only thing they fought over. My dad didn't drink on a regular basis, but he did binge, and when he did, all hell broke loose in my home. My mom tried everything to get him to stop. Everything was fine most of the time, but when those binges came, life was impossible, sad, turned upside down. My brothers were already grown and gone, so I witnessed quite a lot without the support of siblings to lean on. To this day that certain smell of alcohol haunts me, a silent warning.

My mom always said, "You can talk about it inside the house, but once outside, never tell anyone that your father has this problem."

Holding this in, I suffered a lot in school. I should have been a stronger student, but my teachers never knew about the many times throughout the years that there was no time for homework or studying because of the disruption inside my home. My mom would always bring me into the middle of it. The most difficult times were when she'd drive me to a bar when I was as young as ten to try to coax my dad to come home. She'd pull up to a rather seedy bar and insist I go in to get him. I pleaded with her to not make me do it, but she said I was the only one he'd come home for. It was a sickening feeling, walking from the bright outside into a very dark, narrow room with men sitting on bar stools, drunk. I hated seeing my dad like that, and the minute he laid eyes on me, it was clear how hurt and humiliated he was to have me witness his losing struggle with this demon. Naturally, he was furious with my mom for pushing me to go into such a place, but he'd always come out with me, stumbling and squinting as he faced the bright afternoon light, his cheeks rosy from too much alcohol. I would always be crying, scared, embarrassed, wishing this wasn't happening. Hating my dad for being like this. Hating my mom for charging me with this unbearable task.

I still feel the power of her saying, *"Never tell."* And here I am telling. But it's important for me to explain that even at a young age, I understood that this wasn't my dad; this was his drinking problem. He didn't want this. He couldn't help it. He loved me and was a wonderfully caring father. He called me his baby doll, and I adored him. Many years later, it felt strangely ironic to hear my husband, Don, call me "baby doll," never knowing that my dad had called me that. He was such a gentle person, a good provider, but not the strongest person in the world. Drinking was his Achilles' heel, and he was unable to get a grip on it until the latter part of his life.

My high school years were probably no different from my peer's, other than the drama being played out at home with my dad's drinking problem. I went to Marymount High School, an all-girls Catholic School near UCLA. Starting kindergarten at four, a year early, made me one of the youngest in my class every year, but I didn't feel out of place with my older peers. The only time the age difference really bothered me was when my friends could drive or date a year earlier than I could. I never felt that was fair. My parents said I had to be sixteen. They caved a little and moved the timing up to fifteen-and-a-half when I started dating my first boyfriend, Ernie Wolfe, who's still a close friend of mine today.

It's rather funny to think that I was not allowed to go steady in high school for fear I'd get married too young, but I ended up being the youngest of all my friends to marry. My mom didn't want me to marry young like she did, so there was a strict rule in my household that I could only date the same boy once a week. I will say, this gave me an opportunity and great excuse to date a lot of different guys. There was even a stint with Mark Harmon of *NCIS*. I never felt being in a girls' school all day hindered my opportunity to meet eligible guys—there were a number of boys' schools in the vicinity with plenty of young men on the lookout for us. They seemed to be everywhere. Hanging out in the school parking lots after school, dance mixers on a regular basis, brothers of classmates who always seemed to be home with their friends when my girlfriends and I went to one another's homes after school. Dino, Desi and Billy—a '60s singing group comprised of the son of Desi Arnaz and Lucille Ball, Dean Martin's son, and the brother-in-law of one of the Beach Boys—even came to our school mixers. It was an idealistic and innocent time of my life that I will always look back on with wonderful memories.

Even if I did feel a little stifled at an all-girls school, once I turned eighteen I could finally meet my true love on *The Dating Game*. It seemed like everyone who was anyone in Hollywood went on at least one date that way. I thought, *What the heck?* and applied. Being accepted was a fun distraction from home problems, and who knew what could happen? The possibilities were endless and exciting.

"From Hollywood, the dating capital of the world, in color. It's *The Dating Game*. And here's the star of the show and your host, Jim Lang."

Johnny Jacobs' familiar voice was announcing one of the most popular game shows of the '60s as host Jim Lang swiftly bound onto the stage. The audience's enthusiasm veiled their exhaustion from waiting hours outside the stage door to snag a seat. My modeling career throughout high school left little to write home about, but I did have a resume of print work, TV commercials, and a small part on a short-lived series called *The Visual Girl*. As a member of AFTRA, I knew I'd get paid at least $300.00 to be on *The Dating Game*, and maybe I'd even get an interesting date. It was the money and recognition I was looking for more than the date. Secretly I hoped to be "discovered." What the heck? My life at home was pretty grim, and this was my chance to be on television.

Offstage I was nervously awaiting my entrance as each of the three bachelors were being introduced with silly stories, each one more ridiculous than the previous one. I randomly picked my bachelor. On a scale of 1 to 10, he was a 4, and our prize was a trip to New Orleans. What in the world was I going to do with a Mister Four–type in New Orleans?

"Kathi, hi." I had hoped the studio lost my number, but a few days later, Mister Four called. "This is Paul, the guy you met on *The Dating Game*."

After a few pleasantries and an awkward conversation, I knew we weren't going anywhere—most importantly New Orleans. A dinner was one thing, but a whole weekend? Chaperone or no, it wasn't happening. I explained to the representative of the show that my mom was ill, and I really couldn't leave her. Lucky Mister Four still got his prize, and he even got to take someone of his choice.

During the summer between my senior year of high school and freshman year of college, my mom was diagnosed with colon/rectal cancer. It was hard to comprehend because she was always so strong, so full of life, so in charge of the family. I had no idea what it meant, but reality hit pretty quickly.

I just wanted to be normal like my friends. As a teenager, that meant a mom who wasn't ill. After her chemotherapy sessions, my mom and I often stopped at the Brentwood Mart for lunch. It was a nice way to perk up otherwise somber days. The Mart then, and still today, is a small cluster of shops, restaurants, and a specialty grocery store housed in a number of quaint red barn buildings reminiscent of a farmers' market.

Just as I bit into my hamburger, my mom's face went pale and serious as she said, "Kathi, I think I'm going to get sick."

Of all places for her to get sick, I thought, *of course it's one of the most popular hangouts for all my friends.* Before I could say anything, my mom darted from the table, almost knocking into the lady behind us as she pushed her chair back.

I sat there frozen, hoping none of my friends were watching. I kept my head down, staring at my burger and fries in the red-and-white checkered paper basket, as I wondered if my mom had made it to the ladies' room in time. I didn't get up to check. I sat motionless on the little white wooden bench at the picnic table wishing this was happening to someone else's mom, not mine. I had spent so many carefree afternoons there. This time was different; I was different. I had a mom who was throwing up. I looked around to see if any of my friends where there, and I breathed a sigh of relief when I didn't recognize anyone.

She came back and took her place across from me without bringing up her embarrassing escape. My mom never wore much makeup, just a little mascara and lipstick. I noticed how pale she looked. *Would some blush help? Should I mention that?* I silently pondered. No, it would just make her feel like she doesn't look good. She was perspiring as she tried to jump back into the nothing conversation we had been having. I could see beads of sweat gathering on her face. For the first time, she looked vulnerable and frail. This was impossible for me to wrap my head around. My mom was the strongest person I knew.

I have often recalled that afternoon as one of the worst days of my life. Not because of the realization that my mom was ill, but the sickening memory deep in my gut of how I didn't help her. The thought haunted me until years later when I read the book *Motherless Daughters*, by Hope Edelman. I celebrated the discovery that I wasn't alone. My feelings were similar to those of so many motherless women. I was young, immature, and frightened. My mother knew that. She never judged me.

My dad had a very hard time dealing with my mom's diagnosis, and his drinking took on a new fervor. He was trying to escape the reality that the love of his life was facing something so terrible, escape his inability to save her, but mostly, he hated seeing how much more his escape hurt her. He was caught in a Gordian knot. It was still binge drinking, but with more regularity. Needless to say, the two years of my mom's illness were not only extremely difficult, but the sorrow of knowing I was going to lose her was compounded by the sorrow piled on her by my dad's drinking.

More than once she asked me, "Can't he even stop while I'm going through this?"

The answer was no.

He did try. He'd gotten a prescription for some kind of medication that was supposed to squelch his desire for alcohol. One evening, my Mom accused him of having a drink, but he completely denied it. So she put one of the pills in his coffee. She wanted to believe he was telling the truth. And she didn't know that the combination of the pills and alcohol could be lethal. My mom was so weak from her chemo that she couldn't get off the living room sofa when my dad stumbled into the living room gasping for help. He'd lied to her. He had had a drink and was choking to death right in front of us. My mom was wailing and screaming, "He's dying. He's having a heart attack. Call 911!"

In that harrowing moment, I was all alone with the fear that both my parents were about to die right then and there. I called 911. It seemed like an eternity went by, and they weren't showing up. Where were they? We lived up a canyon, and before the days of GPS navigation, our home could be difficult to find. I jumped into my car and raced down our steep driveway onto the narrow, windy canyon road, driving with the fear I wouldn't find help in time to save them. There at the bottom of the canyon were the ambulance and fire engines, lost and turning around on another street. I rolled down my window and yelled, "Follow me."

The paramedics had no idea what they were walking into. My mom on the sofa, half passed out from weakness, fear, and the cancer that was robbing her of her life. My dad barely alive on the carpet in front of her.

"Hurry, please. Hurry!" I struggled to explain in as few words as possible. "My mom is dying of cancer. My father has been poisoned. Please, please, get us to the hospital."

They were both quickly loaded onto gurneys and into the ambulance. Shock and adrenaline blurred the next few minutes, but I followed all alone in my blue Camaro. Driving down that familiar driveway, tears streaming down my cheeks. How could I lose both of my parents tonight?

There was a lot of confusion at the hospital. A lot of questions. My God, I realized, it almost looked as if my mom had poisoned my dad—and she had—but not on purpose. In the ER, surrounded by police asking me questions, I could see one emergency team doing CPR on my dad and another team doing the same on my mom. I called my brothers, and they arrived shortly, thank God. My parents survived the evening, and all misunderstandings were explained, but it was a nightmare that still haunts me.

By the time college rolled around, life was beginning to be a lot different for me than my peers. I wanted to go East for school, but I chose Loyola Marymount not only to be close to home for my mom, but also because it was the alumni of both my brothers, and my parents had been so involved during their time there. The chancellor, Father Casassa, actually baptized me at three weeks old, and my gift from him was to be in the first co-ed class of Loyola University. He felt that by the time I was ready for university, same-sex schools would be obsolete. He was only off by a year.

I enrolled toward the end of summer, toured the campus with my brothers, saw my dorm room, and met my roommate. Within a week, it was clear to me that boarding would be out of the question. My mom was failing and needed me at home, so I was a day student.

Unbeknownst to me, as I was walking across campus my first day, Patrick, a senior, was sitting on a little wall with his buddies checking out all the incoming freshmen girls. He spotted me and said to his friend, "See that girl over there? I'm going to marry her." He went on a quest to find out who knew me. I had no idea any of this was going on, but our first introduction was unforgettable.

I was at a school mixer having fun dancing with a few different guys who were freshmen like me. The band took a break, so I went out onto the patio where Patrick was sitting with a mutual friend. We were introduced and chatted for a while. No question about it—he was adorable. A young look-alike for Brad Pitt. The band started up while we were talking, but he didn't ask me to dance. I loved to dance, and still do, and was beginning to feel a little uncomfortable with little more to say to him, so what was my exit?

"I'll be right back," I said. "I'm going to get a drink of water." I never went back because someone else asked me to dance. I was being spun around the room without a problem in the world, a beautiful and welcomed respite from the sad secret deep in my heart of the problems waiting for me at home. Patrick wasn't used to being ditched, and I heard later he wasn't happy that I had done it.

Within a week, my phone rang.

"Hi, Kathi? It's Patrick. I was just calling to say I have tickets to the Jefferson Airplane concert. I was wondering if you'd like to go with me."

"Wow." I was elated. "Yes."

"That's great. The concert is on October 31, Halloween. I can't wait."

There was a party at Patrick's after the concert. I felt uneasy not knowing anyone. Patrick was a senior, and so were most of his friends. None of the other girls—the other dates—paid much attention to me, and Patrick spent most of the time on the telephone. I finally motioned to him I had to leave. He got off the phone and said, "Sorry, I was talking to my mom."

How stupid does this guy think I am?, I thought. *Of course it was another girl.* I couldn't wait to get home.

I don't know why I said yes to another date. Probably because he was a cute, athletic senior. It was strange to be out of my comfort zone of familiar high school friends. I guess that's how every new freshman feels, but that didn't make it any easier.

We had dated only two months when he called me on his birthday, December 23, from his parents' home in Riverside to tell me he had just told his dad that if we were still dating by June, we'd get married. I had no idea how to respond. I was shocked. He continued on to say if we weren't dating by June, we'd never see one another again. I really don't remember how I answered him. I think I was caught between the disbelief of never experiencing this kind of a threat, and, wow, this sounds pretty cool. We continued to date, but now our conversations included talks of married life, what we'd do when we grew up. I was living a roller coaster of emotions because, when I wasn't in class or with Patrick, I was taking care of my mom. I certainly wasn't thinking clearly with the problems I was experiencing. I had no idea if I was in love. I kept wondering what it was supposed to feel like.

The Vietnam War was in full force, and guys we knew were being drafted left and right. The lottery for the draft came up, and Patrick's number indicated that he was certain to be drafted. To avoid that, he went straight to the local National Guard office and enlisted. Within months, he was sent to Fort Ord near Monterey, California, for six-month boot camp. We wrote to one another almost every day. Was I falling in love through his letters? Or because I couldn't see him? Or because I was so sad at home and didn't know what life had in store for me? Whatever the reasons were, I was eighteen and way too young to be thinking about being married, and Patrick was on a quest to move on to a new life of marriage and family. Patrick would visit as often as he could for quick weekends, and my parents took me to Monterey to visit him a couple of times. On one of those visits Patrick formally proposed at the end of a beautiful street in Carmel overlooking the ocean. From that moment forward, the train was on the track and traveling fast.

I barely saw Patrick during his six-month duty, but throughout this separation, the wedding planning was in full motion. My girlfriends were all excited. My guy friends thought it was a ridiculous idea. Two of them would take me out together knowing I was engaged, but if there were two we all agreed it didn't count as a date. One showed up at my parents' home one day with a present for my mother and then proceeded to suggest to her that I might be too young to get married.

The timing, the reasons, the everything was all wrong. I knew it deep down, but was too fragile or scared to do anything about it. I was living in a constant swirl of emotions. I so wanted my mom to see me as a bride. What little girl doesn't? It weighed on my mind constantly. It was the most important part of my getting married. I just had to have my mom at my wedding, and she was getting sicker and sicker. The excitement, the parties, and the preoccupation throughout it all were most likely what gave my mom a few more months of life. She was so weak before various wedding showers, but she wouldn't miss a single one. My brother made a bed in the back of his station wagon so she could lay down and sleep on the way home from our engagement party. I don't know how she did it, but as much as I wanted her there for the biggest day of my life, she must have been thinking the same thing. We went to Bullock's Wilshire to pick my wedding dress. The store is long gone now, but back then, it was the store of choice. Looking at myself in the mirror with my mom smiling at my side, I felt like a princess, like Guinevere of Camelot.

There was barely any time to spend alone with Patrick once he came home from basic training. We were both still in school, and the wedding preparations and parties were taking over our lives. We barely knew one another.

Two weeks before the wedding, Patrick told me he had had second thoughts about getting married a few days earlier. His dad took him fishing, and after their afternoon together, he got home looking forward to our marriage. This revelation put all sorts of thoughts in my head, but most importantly it made me stop and think. I sat in my bedroom for hours thinking how to explain my thoughts to my mom. I finally found the courage. I walked into her room and sat down next to her. She was lying in bed and had lost so much weight. Her coloring wasn't good, but she still had that wonderful motherly smile for me.

"Mom, I don't think I should marry Patrick. I really don't know him; I've barely spent time with him. I've known him less than a year, and for six months of that time he was away for his National Guard boot camp. Mom, I'm just a kid."

My mother would hear of none of it. "This is normal," she said. "You're just having cold feet. Patrick's a wonderful young man. We like his family. He'll take care of you. Plus, we've had all the parties. You're getting married."

I couldn't argue with her. How could I? She was dying, and we both had the same dream—that she would be at my wedding. Looking back now as an adult, I think my mom was worried about who would take care of me more than anything. My father had his drinking problem, my brothers had their own lives, and she knew life was going to be difficult for me. She wanted to die knowing I was going to be taken care of.

That was that. What else can I say? I was stuck, but maybe it'd be a good stuck.

The wedding was beautiful, and I was happy. Really, really happy and excited to be a bride and a wife. My mom made it and looked beautiful. My two brothers walked her down the aisle, which naturally brought many tears, knowing what a struggle it was for her to make the biggest day of her daughter's life. I walked down the aisle on my father's arm. He had tears streaming down his face. Then I spotted Patrick waiting to take my hand. He looked so handsome. He had tears too. Everyone seemed to be crying, but they were all truly tears of happiness. I knew I was making the right decision. All the prior anxiety had flown away. I had never been so happy or so excited.

There was Father Casassa on the altar. The same priest who'd baptized me. My girlfriends and nieces were the most beautiful bridesmaids of any I had ever seen, but then again, they were the first I'd ever seen. None of my friends had married yet. Their dresses were light yellow in an organza fabric with clusters of small white embroidered flowers. The reception was at the Hotel Bel Air, still one of the most chic hotels in Los Angeles today. Patrick and I walked over the small bridge to the garden where white swans were floating by as we took our family photos. Everyone's always loved the picture of my dad standing alone with his pockets inside out as if the wedding had taken all his money.

A month into our marriage, I got pregnant. It came as an utter surprise to me how easily that could happen. My family used to tease me and say, "Our bags are packed. If the baby comes one day before nine months, we're moving out of town." Times were certainly different back then. When I told my mom, though, her response was something I wasn't prepared for. "You know," she said, "many times it's false. Or the baby doesn't last into the third month."

I hid my disappointment, but secretly I was crushed. I hurried quietly to my old bedroom where I laid down and cried. I was devastated and so hurt that my mom didn't seem to feel the joy I was feeling, that she couldn't feel even a little bit of happiness that might take our minds off of the sorrow of her life coming to an end.

I couldn't understand why my mom would say such a thing to me, why she was acting like there would be no baby. Looking back with more years of wisdom than I had then, I think she knew she'd never meet my baby, and initially, that realization was too painful. She just didn't want to believe that her baby, her little girl, was going to have a grandbaby she'd never meet.

A week went by, and the topic of my pregnancy never came up. Then one day, she handed me a little present.

"What's this?" I asked.

"Open it," she said with a gentle smile.

As sick and exhausted as she was, she had gone shopping and bought my first baby's first present: a little yellow and white layette set, one of the most cherished gifts I have ever received. She looked at me with so much love in her eyes, those dark brown eyes the color of olives.

"I bought this for your baby to wear home from the hospital after he or she is born," she said. And not only did each of my three children eventually wear it home, but all of my grandchildren have too.

Within the last few fleeting months of my mom's life, I almost lost my baby. I had been spending most of my days with my mom as her cancer became increasingly virulent. I lay alone on my parents' bed hoping and praying I wouldn't lose my baby or my mother. I had been bleeding quite a bit, and the doctor was convinced I was having a miscarriage. My father and brother were home, but my mom was at the doctor's receiving the news that she was reacting unfavorably to her latest round of unbearable chemotherapy. She had no idea I was there or that I could hear her from where I was. My brother Don was in the entrance hall, my father close by in the living room. She walked into the house, and with a chilling voice drenched in so much pain, she said the doctor had informed her that there was nothing more that could be done; she probably wouldn't live much longer.

"Mom," I heard Don say, "Kathi is in your room. We think she's losing her baby." She was at my side within minutes, putting all her problems and fears behind her, a character trait that I admired and have carried with me throughout my life. With all the Irish fire she could muster, she launched into an unbelievable course of taking care of me. She had no idea I had overheard her unbearable news, and I never let on that I did. As her fire cooled to a smolder, she crawled into bed with me where we stayed together for most of the next couple weeks. We didn't talk about her problem or mine; we just moved forward with life. Maybe it's the Irish way of doing things—not talking or baring one's soul, but digging into what needs to be done and silently giving support from one's heart. We reveled in the bittersweet opportunity to be together and feel how much we loved one another and never faltered from our positive attitudes that we would both get better.

My mom wanted to be home as long as possible. She tried her hardest, but the week she died, she told us all, "I think it's time to go to the hospital." I followed the ambulance from our home to St. John's Hospital in Santa Monica. I was driving the car behind and could see her looking at me through the window. I made gestures and pointed out some of the new things that had happened on our little street in Sullivan Canyon with only a handful of homes. I knew as I did this it would be the last time she would ever be there, and I wanted her to remember it smiling. Off we went down the street she drove so many times. *The street she always drives way too fast on*, I couldn't help but to think with a tearful half-smile.

I sat outside her room in the waiting area, frequently walking in to sit by her side. I was so scared. I didn't want her to see me crying, because I felt it would be a giveaway that her end was coming. She had worked so hard and didn't want to give up. I didn't want to be the one to fracture her spirit. I was so incredibly scared and sad. I finally walked into her room and chose a spot in the corner. A place where I could watch her, but a distance far enough away that she wouldn't see my fear. As she came and went from consciousness, recognizing friends and family, I stayed back. I was scared to be so close to the love of my life knowing that she was about to be taken from me. I was barely nineteen and pregnant with my first baby; I could not lose my mother. How was I supposed to grow as an adult and a mother without the strongest, most interesting woman I had ever known? I didn't think I could make it through, and I didn't want to. I didn't want to lose her.

I knew the end was coming, and I quietly took my spot next to her, looking into her eyes as she gently passed on to eternity. It is a hurt that lies deep within me and still brings fresh tears to my eyes so many decades later.

I cried myself to sleep that night in the arms of my husband, thinking it was impossible for me to be happy again. I finally glided into an unconscious realm far away from my sadness, far away from the realities of my life, far away from how I was going to forge ahead without the strength and stability of the strongest appendage of my own soul.

I jolted awake to the unmistakable feeling of my baby kicking for the first time. It was the first signs of life I had felt from my baby and the first time I had felt any kind of happiness for what seemed like eons. My mom was looking out for me, sending me a message with every little kick. *Kathi, life goes on. You're now the mother. You have a life that depends on you. It's time for you to move forward, take that life and not look back.* She never sent me another sign, but I still think back to that message in times of need. From that night on, I was in charge. It was time for me to be the woman she dreamed I would be. I had to embrace life and cherish my future and the futures of my loved ones, no matter how impossible the challenge I was facing. I made a conscious choice to recognize the gift of a new life and its infinite possible paths. It was time to fill my heart with this new, unpredictable journey.

My dad tried so hard, but those first few months were impossible for him. I never realized how hard he had it until I was widowed and learned for myself what the loss of a spouse really is. How deep it is. How profound. The quiet nights, the constant pit in the stomach, the pain that just won't go away. Waking in the middle of the night and seeing an unused pillow. He ended up in the hospital with the symptoms of a mini stroke from his excessive drinking. My brothers and I got him back home, but more of the same challenges ensued. It was a lot to handle on top of being freshly motherless, newly married, and expecting my first baby.

The day the baby finally came, I was staying with my brother Don, because my husband, Patrick, was fulfilling his National Guard duties that weekend. Early in the morning, I was awakened by a sharp pain in my back. I went to my brother's room and told him I thought I was going into labor, but he didn't think so and told me to go back to sleep. It took a while to convince him. We called my husband at the barracks in Riverside, and he immediately got permission to leave his weekend duties, jumped in his car, and got to me as quickly as he could. Once again, we headed off to St. John's Hospital.

"Give me drugs, please," I begged. "Why would anyone ever do this again? Please, more drugs."

Jennifer was born, and my life changed forever. It was no longer about me, about the grief I was feeling from the death of my mother or anything life-threatening in the world. It was about my beautiful little baby girl. "My little Jennifer." Not sure why I started calling her that, or why I still do, but whenever I think of her, "my little Jennifer" comes to mind. I had guessed she would be a girl and there she was, all purple and crying—a gift from the heavens.

Being the first of all my friends to be married and have a baby was quite a novelty, so it was a revolving door of curiosity and excitement. The waiting room was overflowing with family and friends. My brothers, sister-in-law Barbara (the only sister I've ever had), my nieces and nephews, girlfriends, Patrick's family. There were probably close to forty in all.

I had a roommate at the hospital, and the poor thing was miserable, in her forties and overwhelmed with her "late in life, surprise baby." She had to put up with my fan club of visitors. The giggles from my girlfriends. The tears of happiness from my husband. The inexperienced questions I bombarded her with. Wherever she is today, I owe her a lunch. Oh my, she'd be in her eighties by now.

All went well until the middle of the night. I felt my neck. It had swollen practically to the width of my shoulders. When I touched it, it sounded like I was popping plastic bubble wrap. I showed the nurse who came in, and she panicked, which scared me. Within minutes there was a team of doctors at my bedside examining me, then rushing me off to be X-rayed. During childbirth, I had experienced a spontaneous pneumothorax. An air pocket in my lung burst, dispensing air outside of my lung and into my chest cavity. The doctors worried this would put pressure on my lung and cause it to collapse. They watched it for a few days as the air pocket slowly healed itself and the air dissipated. I was too naive to be alarmed, but I was sad. I wanted my mom.

One night, a nurse walked into my room and spotted me quietly crying.

"What do you have to cry about?" she asked curtly. "You have a healthy baby. The girl down the hall just lost her baby."

Eyes filled with tears, I said, "My mom just died a couple of months ago. And my dad is in the hospital across the street because of a severe drinking problem. I have no parents right now, and I feel so alone. I just want my mom."

The nurse left the room quickly, and I never saw her again. I have no idea how she felt, but I learned that night that things aren't always as they seem. Judgment of others is never fair, and it's usually inaccurate if you're basing it only on what you see. There is always so much more to the story.

Initially, life was devastating after my mom's death. I longed to call her and ask her about all the silly little things that are so important in an everyday relationship between a mother and her teenage daughter. How do you make baked apples? Where did you pack my ski clothes? What's the name of the lady at the cleaners? The hardest questions were the ones a first-time mother would ask. What do I do now? Is it normal for her to cry like that? Did I do such-and-such when I was a baby, too? Answers I'd never get. She'd never be there to answer the phone. She'd never be there to be my friend. I'd never have the chance to be on equal footing with her. To see what it would be like to be an adult with her and not the child she had so constantly watched over.

Beyond all the drama, I finally arrived home with little Jennifer. What a blessing and diversion she was from the death of my mother five months earlier. Patrick and I had taken classes at the Red Cross on how to feed, change, and bathe a baby, but we still felt so unprepared. Little Jennifer wasn't like the plastic baby dolls we practiced on. She cried. She screamed. She had colic. I had a lot to learn, but Little Jennifer was the beginning of the rest of my life.

My dad was released from the hospital about six weeks after my baby was born. I had planned to meet him at a home he had rented at the beach. He insisted on getting there first and readying the place with groceries for Little Jennifer and me. Patrick was to follow in a few days. I was looking forward to a new beginning with my dad, but when I walked into the little beach cottage, I found him passed out on the couch. I ran out with my baby to my friend Bootsie's home a few blocks away. I told her mom what had happened, and I was immediately welcomed to stay the week with them. My brothers came and took our dad back to the hospital. I was so incredibly hurt, but I know my dad was upset, too. He didn't mean for that to happen. He really didn't. But it did.

This was the first time I'd shared with anyone the problem of my dad's drinking—echoes of my mother's "never tell"s in the back of my mind. I had known this family all through high school. Bootsie was one of my best friends but never knew what was going on behind my closed door.

They say one has to hit rock bottom before they can really get up, and that's exactly what happened to my dad. That was the last time I ever saw him drink. Leaving the beach house, he was so violently ill, so defeated, so ashamed. He reached a tipping point and somehow managed to pull himself together. Finally. After all those years. So much longer than any of us had hoped—and too late for my mom—but he did it.

I have always tried to find positives out of terrible situations. It's something my mom instilled in me, and I try to instill in my children. It's bizarre to think this, but the positive part of my mom's death was that it catalyzed the truly close bond that formed between myself and my father. Yes, I loved him through thick and thin, but my mom was always the strength of the family. She was the one who stood out like the North Star. My dad was sometimes lost in the galaxy. It's strange to think of it this way, maybe, but he finally had a chance to shine.

Life was still hard, though. We had an amazing support system, but Patrick and I still struggled as young newlyweds and brand new parents. I never thought owning a washer and dryer would mean so much to me, especially at the age of nineteen, but boy did it. Patrick and I were married a mere month when I became pregnant.

"Do you think we should do something about me not getting pregnant right away?" I shyly asked Patrick on our honeymoon.

"We don't need to worry about that. It's not that easy. You can only get pregnant one hour of the month, and the chances we hit that are one in a million," he answered as the confident husband I knew I had married. Albeit twenty-one years old and obviously not very experienced with the ways of the world.

There I was, nine months later, little Jennifer in the car seat as we hauled off to the laundromat with my car loaded with laundry, and a bag of diapers in the trunk. Not Pampers, I might add, but the real thing. Who would have thought? My friends were going to sorority parties in college, and I was deep in laundry with a jar full of change, reading movie magazines while I waited for the spin cycle to stop, rocking a baby who should really be in her crib taking a nap.

"Patrick," I excitedly shouted as he opened the door to our tiny second-floor apartment. "I have a great idea. I know we can't afford a washer and dryer, but how about if you go on a game show and win one?"

"What? Are you nuts?" he answered.

"No, seriously," I quickly answered without telling him I had already submitted his name for the TV show *Hollywood Squares* and he had been accepted.

"Well, what the heck," he answered with more of a grimace than a smile.

He was getting used to my "creative ideas." Never having a dull moment seems to be a theme that has followed me throughout life.

The anticipated day came with much fanfare from our family and friends with a party being planned upon our return. My dad said he'd babysit little Jennifer so I wouldn't have to amuse her in the audience while Patrick was being "My Star" of the *Hollywood Square* stars.

"Patrick, which square do you choose?" asked the host, Paul Lynde.

"I'll take square number one," Patrick answered nervously. Paul looked at Charlie Weaver sitting in the top left square and asked the first question. Charlie answered with a somewhat ridiculous answer. The cameras focused on Patrick, and without a second of hesitation, he said, "No, Charlie's wrong."

"Yeah! He got it right," I squealed as the audience applauded.

"One down, two to go, Patrick. Where to next?" Paul asked.

"I'd like square number four." It was directly under his first square. I don't remember the question, but I do remember Patrick won the square easily. Two down, one to go. We were on track for life on Easy Street. *Please Patrick, don't goof. This is it! This is so easy. I can already see the water swirling and the dryer spinning.*

"I'll take square number five in the middle with Zsa Zsa Gabor."

What's he doing? I nervously thought as I gnawed on my nails. *Doesn't he know how to play tic-tac-toe?*

A disappointed hum came over the audience as Paul Lynde said, "That's an interesting strategy, Patrick." The question was asked. Something about nursery rhymes. Of course it didn't matter what Ms. Gabor answered or what Patrick said. The game was over, and in a blink of an eye, we were quietly driving home.

"Why didn't you go to the square on the bottom?" I had to ask, even though it was a daring proposition.

"I know, I know," he shot back, exasperated. "I was so nervous being on television, and the squares were so close to me that I could hardly figure out which one was which."

Even back then, I knew it wasn't worth worrying about things that couldn't be changed, so I switched gears now that my curiosity was satisfied.

"Guess what, Patrick?" I exclaimed. "They gave us an iron as a consolation prize!"

Patrick tried, and I could certainly relate to being overwhelmed. Deep in my heart, I really wanted him to be my knight in shining armor, but alas, he asked Zsa Zsa Gabor. I knew that I could have nailed it if I'd been the contestant, but as a member of the Screen Actors Guild, I was ineligible.

Despite our brief moments of fame, our family and friends were there to celebrate our iron and ask all about the experience of being on set. I loved the iron-strong bond we shared with our families regardless of our successes and hardships.

The last few years of my father's life were a complete joy for me. When little Jennifer was about a year and half old, Patrick had a job opportunity with his father in Missouri, so we moved there. "Kathi," my dad told me, "people don't move that way; they move *this* way." He was astounded that I was moving from California to Missouri. It was only supposed to be a two-year stint, but we ended up staying for nine. I went kicking and screaming, but it enriched my life with lifelong friends, happiness and heartbreak, and a lifestyle few of my friends have experienced.

For the first time in my life, I was making friends outside of my native security of Los Angeles, and as I settled in, I felt like I was in a very special place. For one thing, our first home in comparison to Los Angeles prices was a dream come true. It was a beautiful little English Tudor stone house with a slate roof. My brother Don and I found it by him knocking on the door and asking them if they'd be interested in selling. I was so embarrassed that I hid on the floor of the car. Next thing you knew, Patrick and I owned the house and were moving in.

After we moved, my dad would visit for weeks at a time. He'd take care of little Jennifer while I played tennis with my girlfriends. He had a great rapport with my husband. He was frequently welcomed into my friends' homes. Life was good. He was my buddy. He was even there for the birth of my son.

Kevin came two years, nine months after little Jennifer. I had just filmed a commercial for a local beauty salon, and it was going to be shown at our favorite movie theater. I was supposed to look sexy, peeking through a chiffon scarf, but I felt like I looked anything but. Patrick and I were at the movies with our friends when the commercial came on—right before *The Exorcist*. I was so embarrassed. I thought I looked ridiculous in the commercial and hoped no one surrounding us would recognize me, now a pregnant girl, as the same person. I never knew if it was my embarrassment over the commercial or the intensity of the movie, but something sent me into labor, and the four of us left early and hurried to the hospital.

This birth was quicker, albeit so quick the anesthesia didn't have time to kick in. Once again I was begging the familiar refrain, "Give me drugs! I don't care what you have, just give me something." Within a blink of an eye, we had a baby boy.

"My son, I have a son." Of course, proud Dad was over the moon. I think he was ready to take Kevin fishing that night.

I prepped Little Jennifer about the forthcoming baby, hoping she wouldn't be jealous with this new little creature taking some of her mommy and daddy's time from her. "I need your help. You're going to help me with your baby brother, let's do it together." From that day forward, Jennifer got the title "JM" for Junior Mom. She never got jealous because she had a job to do. If I was changing Kevin's diapers, Jennifer was handing me the Pampers.

She took her role very seriously, but went a little overboard one evening. I was in the kitchen, and Little Jennifer walked in holding three-month-old Kevin under her arm like a football, announcing, "Mommy, the baby is hungry."

"Jennifer," I said, practically frozen with concern, "walk slowly and hand Kevin to me."

She had crawled into his crib, taken him out—I dare not imagine how—walked down a flight of stairs, across the hardwood floor of our living room, and into the kitchen.

Unfortunately, soon after Kevin was born, my dad was diagnosed with throat cancer. He just couldn't give up those cigarettes. I regularly flew back and forth between California and Missouri to take care of him. Each time, I would pack up the kids and set up the playpen in his apartment. I sat with him day after day, pureeing his food in the blender to make it easier to swallow. I felt guilty leaving my young husband back in Missouri, and each time I left my dad, I felt guilty leaving him alone in California. I was in a constant state of "the guilts," but I knew where I really needed to be. My dad was ill, and he needed me. It was a precursor to the deep guilt I felt many years later as a caregiver to my husband after his stroke. I wasn't aware back then, but it's an incredibly common emotion for caregivers of all ages.

I would bundle my dad up, put the babies in the car, and drive them all around Los Angeles. Past his old school, which had been turned into a factory. Past my godparents' house at Lake Sherwood, where my parents spent idle days at their best friends' lake home filled with everyone's families. Up into the San Bernardino mountains to see the cabin at Lake Arrowhead where he and my mom raised my brothers each summer. On and on and on. Road trips to his past. A history of his life. I felt so lucky to have this time with him.

He was in agony and would drink a swig of codeine when the pain was too much.

"Dad," I'd say, "you've got to quit smoking."

"Why? I'm dying. Why should I give up my last pleasure in life?"

I guess he had a point.

The doctors felt his cancer was curable and were trying radiation, but he needed surgery to determine if it had spread to his lungs. His heart was in bad shape, however, so there was the fear that even if the cancer could be removed, he might not make it through surgery.

He stood at the end of the driveway waiting to say goodbye to me. I knew I'd never see him again, and I knew he felt the same. I couldn't see him clearly through the window; it could've been from rain or because I was crying so hard. I looked at him in the rearview mirror. He stood all alone, waving as I disappeared down the long driveway, tears rolling down his cheeks.

When I got home, I called and pleaded with him. "Please, Dad, give it a chance. You don't have much time without the surgery. Why not try?"

"Kathi," he said, "I've had a good life. I don't want to take the chance of leaving today if the surgery doesn't work. I miss your mom, and I'm ready to go, but I don't want to go today." He chose to not do the surgery.

Wrapping one's head around a loved one's choice can feel impossible, and for me, my father's decision seemed so obviously wrong at first. As the caregivers being left behind, it aches to our very core when a loved one decides it's their time But their reasoning is right for them, and once I was able to grasp that, I was able to make the most of the time we had left. Living life on our own terms is something we strive for and encourage, but we often overlook the flip side of that idea that our palliative care should be on our own terms as well. My father made the decision that was right for him, and it wouldn't have improved his quality of life or our last precious opportunities to connect if I'd argued any further. Support and love were the best things I could give him, and I won't pretend like that made it any easier for me, but I hope it made it easier for him.

One morning in 1974, years after his Air Force career, and now the father of five children, my brother Dink could barely get out of bed. Normally his health was exceptional; he even won an award in high school for never missing a day of school. My brother Don called and told me Dink was on his way to the hospital in an ambulance. The reality just couldn't resonate with me.

"It must be a fluke," I said to my brother on the other end of the phone. "No way can he be ill. He never gets sick." By this time, I was living in Springfield, Missouri, with my husband and my two children. The distance quickly felt like a million miles. The thought of my brother on his way to the hospital left me with a queasy, frightened feeling in my stomach. I couldn't help but to think about seeing my mother in the ambulance as we left home for the last time. A few days of waiting for test results stretched out into infinity. At first, doctors thought he had leukemia. We were all devastated by the news. The word chemo was no longer convincing to me. It didn't work for my mom, so why would I trust it could work for my brother?

"Hello, Kathi. I have some news about Dink that you need to hear." My brother Don had sat in on the doctor's meeting with our sister-in-law, Barbara, and Dink and had called to fill me in. I steeled myself. "He doesn't have leukemia, but he does have what they're calling aplastic anemia of the bone marrow."

"What's that?" I struggled to reconcile the wonderful news that it wasn't cancer with this new, unfamiliar phrase that left a knot deep in my stomach.

"All I really know is that the doctors said it's when your bone marrow doesn't make enough blood cells. They said it was extremely rare and was the result of being poisoned." A palpable silence weighed down the line and settled between us.

"What could possibly have poisoned him?" I barely breathed.

"No one knows." I could feel Don gearing up to tell me the hard part. "Right now, all that matters is how serious this is. His only chance of survival is a bone marrow transplant. Our bone marrow produces our blood, so the blood transfusions will keep him alive in the short term until a donor can be found."

It was later determined that his condition was a result of exposure to radiation while in the Air Force. We knew that he'd be gone days at a time flying secret missions, but the specifics were always far above the clearance granted to worried, loving family members. Family folklore has it that he flew his F-84F Thunderstreak into Red China, but we'll never know if that's true. Even now, it's hard to imagine a career he loved so much turning on him so cruelly.

Today, one's chances of survival from aplastic anemia are higher with the aid of internet resources to millions of people and the National Marrow Registry's tens of thousands of donors, but in 1974 the only way to find a perfect donor was digging through old-fashioned medical records. Finding a perfect match was as lucky as finding a needle in a haystack. The best chance would be an identical twin, which he didn't have. The next closest chance would be a sibling.

I immediately flew to Los Angeles to see him. He was weak. His color was terrible, but he was tackling the problem like a business situation. Reading everything he could get his hands on, talking to a multitude of doctors, tackling each treatment and update like a fourth-quarter comeback. He would win. The team would win. The family would win.

I went to UCLA to be tested as a donor. My brother Don had already done so, but he didn't match closely enough. Dink met me at the top of the stairs outside the parking lot to the hospital. He gave me a hug and thanked me a million times for coming. He explained how important the transplant was, but apparently how difficult it would be for me as a donor to go through if we matched closely enough. He wanted me to completely understand how painful it would be for me and how much he would understand if I didn't want to do it. I just knew it would be me who would save his life. My brother would live, and he would finally see me as the woman I matured to, not as his bratty little sister. This was my chance to save his life. I loved him, and now we would be forever bound through life with a closeness few could ever have. He would receive my bone marrow, which would regenerate in him, giving him a new chance at life.

After a blood test to check DNA markers for compatibility, he sat me down and told me we didn't match closely enough. He was so disappointed. I had never before seen my fighter pilot brother, star athlete and now successful businessman, with the look of such utter defeat. I think it was the first time I ever saw tears in his eyes and maybe the only time. I was devastated. I couldn't save my brother's life.

My brother taught me how to live life through the face of adversity. He tackled each day as if the impossible was inevitable. He barely missed a day of work no matter how ill he felt. He spent nights in the hospital, hooked up to an IV with pint after pint of blood filling his veins, and then go into work with nary a complaint, as if everything was normal. It was a grueling couple of years, but he lived with the optimism that a donor would be found, and in the meantime, he would fight to be strong and live his life as normally as possible.

Arthur "Dink" Robinson and his wife, Barbara

He had taken his four older children on a trip around the US many years earlier, with me as part of the gang. He wanted to do the same for his youngest child, who was too young at the time to make the trip. The doctors said it would be impossible, but he called every major hospital on his round-the-country tour and arranged through his doctors to take off every few days to receive blood transfusions. Despite the unheard of challenge, his little boy was going to have this trip with him no matter what anyone thought.

The next few years for him were a constant battle to survive. His fight for life was mirroring my father's struggle. No one knew who would go first, but I held on to the dream of a miracle for both of them.

In a bittersweet mercy, my dad passed away on Christmas Eve, 1975. He wouldn't have been able to handle the death of his son.

When my dad elected not to take his chance with surgery, I couldn't understand where he was coming from, but now I do. We celebrate birth; we celebrate all our milestones through life, but the one we run from is death. It's so hard for the ones left behind, but through all the experiences I've had with end of life, I now understand how important it is for one to have their last milestone in life be celebrated. It's a gift to let one go in their own way without the guilt of the patient having to worry about the ones they're leaving behind. It's their time. Yes, it's so hard on everyone else, but it's also a time to celebrate the rich life that person has experienced, whether good or bad, hard or easy.

During the first part of 1976, I suffered from the death of my father. I was deeply depressed but didn't know it. I felt physically sick every day, an uncontrollable reaction to something I couldn't quite put a name to. I lost close to twenty pounds, and needless to say, I looked horrible.

"I'm taking you to the hospital," my husband said one snowy Missouri Sunday. "There's something wrong with you. This isn't normal."

I didn't argue. I knew I had to go. I knew something was wrong. I was in the ER on a gurney when my doctor came in. He was startled to see what I looked like. Patrick explained how sick I had been, and my doctor immediately said, "She needs to be admitted. We need to do some tests. Something's wrong."

I could still hear the whisper of my mom saying to me, *never tell*, but I ignored it and blurted out, "Doctor, I lost my mom a couple of years ago. My dad just died, and my brother doesn't have much longer. My whole family is dying. I'm just so sad."

"Kathi," my doctor said with an unforgettable expression of compassion, "there's nothing wrong with you other than you're about to have a nervous breakdown. No one can go through this kind of stress." He wanted to keep me in the hospital, but I just couldn't bear to stay there. I wanted to go home to my husband and babies. My doctor said OK, but only if I would take some medication to get me through this roller coaster of life, with complete rest at home.

When Dink heard what happened, he called and told me he was coming to Missouri. He didn't want anyone knowing he was coming. He only wanted to see me and talk to my doctor. He didn't like the fact the doctor had prescribed Valium and wanted to find out what was going on. He sounded weak on the other end of the phone. I asked to talk to my sister-in-law. She told me he had pneumonia. I pleaded with him not to come. It was too dangerous. He wouldn't hear of it, saying he had business in New York and would use that as an excuse to see me on his way home to California.

I never talked to him again. He flew to New York and passed out in a coffee shop at the Newark Airport with a high fever. People ignored him, not knowing who he was or what his problem was. They probably thought he was a passed out drunk and not someone they wanted to involve themselves with. Someone finally called an ambulance, and he was transported to the hospital. When the doctors asked who he was, he refused to tell them. He said, "I'm dying. Let me die in peace."

My family is one of complex relationships, and Dink's and mine was no exception. The bond between a younger sister and older brother is a strange and sacred thing. He was tough on me and often hurtful, but in his last years, I saw a glimpse of his lifelong love for me and his respect for me as I grew older. Despite our contentious start, we bonded when faced with life's greatest struggle. I know I am lucky to have witnessed his true strength.

Even in the darkest moments, when I felt like there couldn't possibly be a way to carry on, the earth kept spinning, the days kept passing by, and life continued on. I found out I was pregnant, and a little light flickered on at the end of the tunnel. Nothing could ever replace the family I'd lost, but I knew I'd see their expressions and mannerisms in my precious children as they grew up.

Patrick and I were visiting my brother Don in Hawaii the Christmas before Brooke was born. For some reason, I never showed much during the first trimester of my pregnancies, so I decided not to tell anyone I was pregnant right away. We wanted to wait and surprise Jennifer and Kevin during the holidays. Christmas morning, after the excitement of Santa Claus had worn off, we made the announcement to Jennifer and Kevin that they were going to have a baby brother or sister.

"This is the happiest day of my life!" Jennifer jumped up and shrieked in excitement. At seven and a half, she was a ball of energy. Kevin paid no attention, but at four, nothing was more fun than playing with his new toys.

The day of Brooke's birth came quite unexpectedly. I was at a luncheon with girlfriends six weeks before her due date when my water broke. One friend quickly drove me home, where Patrick was waiting to take me to the hospital. Everything seemed to be going well until the birth. I barely got to see my precious new baby before I was whisked to recovery. Patrick and his mother came in for a few seconds to see me. Patrick seemed anxious, and his mom had tears in her eyes. Something seemed very wrong, but before I could ask what was going on, they were both gone. I lay there alone with all sorts of terrible thoughts filling my imagination. Was everything OK? I silently feared the worst.

A nun I had never met before quietly came in and sat down beside me. She explained that there was a problem. My baby was struggling to breathe because she was born before her lungs fully developed. It would be twenty-four hours before they would know if she had the strength to survive. I begged to see her and was finally wheeled into the nursery. There she was in an incubator. So tiny and battling for each precious breath as her little body arched and fought for life. Patrick had his hands placed through two holes of the incubator, which enabled him to pat her. The doctors explained that many times babies survive just from human touch giving them the will to live. I might have brought her into the world, but Brooke's dad gave her the will to fight as he stayed by her side throughout the night, never leaving her.

Without a doubt, my most successful, difficult, and rewarding profession has been motherhood. Since I was a little girl playing with baby dolls, it was all I ever aspired to be. I didn't want one baby or two; I wanted twelve. My favorite movie growing up was *Cheaper by the Dozen*, the classic film starring Clifton Webb and Myrna Loy. I must have seen it a hundred times, and I wanted a life just like theirs.

While wanting to be a mother, I was no exception to the little girl dreams of modeling and movie stardom. My brother had dated a number of starlets whom he brought to the house from time to time, which only enlivened my dreams.

The local department store ran a contest for an inexperienced young girl to be in their fashion show. I was with my mom buying school clothes, and without mentioning it to her, filled out the form. I won! That afternoon was the beginning of a modest career. I had taken a few modeling classes, but this was definitely different—people were watching me. As my mom and I were leaving the store after my runway debut, a producer named Al Burton invited me to audition for a show he was making called *The Visual Girl,* which was geared towards teenage girls. With a few recommendations from Mr. Burton, I easily found an agent. Modeling for print ads, television commercials, and the show were fun, but it was also very demanding with school and the onset of the infant stages of my mother's illness.

On the set of The Visual Girl

My acting and modeling career came to a halt after Patrick and I moved to Missouri, but I picked it up again when we returned to Los Angeles a decade later. My daughter Jennifer was ten years old and, having grown up seeing photos of some of my work, announced she wanted to be in commercials too. I called Al for advice.

"Kathi, you were always my teenage all-American girl. Now you're the all-American mother. When Jennifer goes on auditions, you ought to try out for the mom parts."

He was right, and for a number of years, I worked alongside each one of my children. McDonald's, Shredded Wheat, Kodak, we loved all the commercials we worked on together.

My true vocational passion was architecture, and if I'd had the opportunity, I would have chosen it as my professional field. Marrying and having babies at such a young age put completing my college degree on the back burner, and when Patrick and I moved to Springfield, Missouri, there wasn't a university close by that taught or offered architecture.

I was first exposed to construction when my parents built their dream home designed by the renowned architect Cliff May. I remember as an eight-year-old looking over the plans with them and being intrigued by how Mr. May's sketches were developing into the home I was going to live in for most of my childhood. As I got older and subscribed to *Seventeen* and *Teen Magazine*, I was also thumbing through house plan magazines at the grocery store, always intrigued with the different styles and dreaming about creating plans of my own.

While pregnant with Brooke, I'd pop the kids in the car and drive through every existing neighborhood in Springfield looking for the perfect buildable lot. "Oh no, not again," Jennifer and Kevin would cry. I had inherited a little money from my parents and wanted to use it to build a speculative house, or "spec house" in the industry lingo. One day I spotted the perfect lot and couldn't wait to get home to tell Patrick all about it.

"Patrick, I found it," I excitedly told him as he walked in from work one evening.

"Daddy, now we don't have to sit in the car all day. Mommy found a lot," said Kevin's tiny voice echoing my enthusiasm.

The expression "ignorance is bliss" found a home with me. Never for a moment did I hesitate or worry about my newfound career. The ink wasn't dry on the purchase contract when I was at the local lumberyard buying a paperback book titled something like *How to Build a House in 10 Easy Steps*. It became my bible.

I met with our local banker who gave me a construction loan. Something which probably wouldn't happen so easily today. As papers were being drawn up, we shared a promise and a friendly handshake; today that would be replaced with mounds of requirements in legal documents.

Jennifer and Kevin loved mommy's job because when not in school they spent the entire day on the job site with me playing on the dirt piles, hammering boards together, and discovering how fun it was to run through a house in framing. Seeing a roofer holding six-month-old Brooke as I climbed up a ladder to inspect his work was the norm, right along with the voice saying, "Kathi, hurry up. The other guys are going to tease me for holding a baby on the job."

"Oh, don't worry. They all do it," I'd laughingly reply. I was Kathi Contractor and loving it.

Every Friday, with baby Brooke on my hip and the other two in tow, I made my weekly construction draw at the savings and loan to pay the subcontractors. My biggest compliment came when the president of the bank called me into his office and said, "Kathi, you are the only builder we have that has come in under budget and on time. Would you consider building out some homes under construction we've foreclosed on?"

I felt a rush of pride and quickly prayed, *Please God, don't let my cheeks turn pink again. It's so embarrassing.* "Thank you so much," I replied, "but with three babies, I don't have the time to take on any more projects. I'd rather stick to one home at a time."

Over the years, I did build several more spec homes in Missouri, and I even ventured down into Mexico when I'd gotten my sea legs. It's a passion I will always foster and one that I'm grateful to have been able to explore and make some money with. I strongly believed that it was good for my children to grow up seeing both their parents work hard and strive to be successful in both their roles as professionals and as parents. And based on the wonderful adults and parents they have become, I will own that we did a pretty darn good job.

I will never regret my twenty-seven years with Patrick. Those years were filled with many wonderful moments and, yes, many challenges. We had three fantastic children together and now share eight grandchildren. It isn't the dozen I'd dreamed of; it's even better. The reality is—Patrick and I were just too darn young, and even a dozen fantastic children wouldn't have made our marriage the right path for us.

My kids are such a reflection of Patrick and me. All our warts and flaws, but they got the good stuff too. It's hard to see my mirror image misbehaving or disagreeing, but I gave them the best thing I possibly could—the strength to disagree and the confidence to put themselves out there, even if it means misbehaving sometimes. I'm so proud of them and the way they are now raising their children. Kevin can be so strict. I tease him that he must know all the stuff I didn't catch.

After Patrick and I divorced, it was a new era for me. My kids were raised, for the most part. The difficult periods of family illnesses and deaths were behind me. It was a new carefree, happy time in my life.

2

UNFORGETTABLE

"And forever more that's how you'll stay."
—Nat King and Natalie Cole

People often ask me where Don Koll and I first met. I was with my family in Cabo San Lucas on vacation and was introduced to him as the owner of the Palmilla Hotel. He stuck so vividly in my memory because of how his kind smile and friendly demeanor made him seem so young. At that time in my life, I envisioned hotel owners as old and stuffy. Over the years, I noticed that he always did look younger than his age. I even remember what he was wearing—a short-sleeved white shirt with khaki pants. It was the late 1980s, and I didn't meet him again for a couple of years. He didn't remember meeting me that first time, but his charisma stayed with me.

Flash forward ten years. I was separated from Patrick and finding my way on my own for the first time in my life. I was lucky to be surrounded by supportive, loving friends and children whose love extended beyond their parents' marriage license.

At the end of an exceptionally exhausting day, I walked into my home and noticed my answering machine blinking. The message was from my friend Barbara Thornhill saying, "Kathi, call me. This is about your love life."

What the heck was she thinking about? I wondered. I was newly separated and not quite ready to think of a "love life." Just as I was about to return her call my phone rang. It was Don Koll. He knew I was going through a divorce and had called me a number of times asking if I needed any advice. I think it was an excuse on his side, and I found out later I was right. He was about to go to an event in Washington, DC, and had called Barbara and her then-husband Gary Wilson to see if he could attend some of the events with them. He had run into them the previous year and thought they would be attending again. Apparently Barbara asked him who his date would be, and he said, "I won't have a date. I'll be alone." Barbara said, "If I were you, I'd ask Kathi Smith. If you don't, someone else will."

Don took the bait. After a few pleasantries he asked, "Isn't your birthday coming up? December seventh, right?"

"Wow. Yes, it is." I was surprised he knew the date, but then again, a lot of people remember my birthday; it's on Pearl Harbor Day, the "day that will live in infamy."

"What are you doing for your birthday?"

"Well, I celebrated it over Thanksgiving with my family, so I haven't made plans yet."

"If you're free, how about going to the White House with me?" he suggested. All I could think was, the White House? There's a restaurant in Laguna Beach called The White House, so my first reaction was to ask which one, but I didn't want him to think the only reason I wanted to go with him was to go to *that* White House. "I'm on the board of trustees of The Kennedy Center, and the seventh is the weekend of The Honors. I've asked another couple from New York to join me, and I think it would be fun if you could come too. You'll have your own room, and you can do whatever you want throughout the weekend. I know my friend's wife wants to shop, but don't feel like you have to do what she wants to do. It's your choice. Other than the Honors, there will be a dinner at the State Department and reception at the White House."

"Thanks," I said, trying to sound cool but feeling nervous and excited. "Can I check a few things out and call you back?" It was December third, and he was talking about the seventh.

I immediately called my son, Kevin and said, "You're not going to believe this, but Mr. Koll has invited me to the White House. What should I do?"

"Mom, you've got to go. You might not ever have the chance to go to the White House again."

That was that. I called Don back after a couple of hours and accepted. He sounded so excited, and I loved his enthusiasm.

I asked Don years later why he chose such a spectacular evening for our first date. He told me he had been thinking about asking me out and wanted to invite me to something he thought I wouldn't turn down, saying, "You know, guys don't like rejection."

I didn't lose time suggesting what I wanted to do. Shopping was out of the question. Why shop in DC when I live in Southern California, which has every store imaginable? "Don, what I'd really like to do is see some of the sights I haven't seen since I was on a seventh grade trip with my brother Don."

Before I knew it, I was in Washington sitting in the back of a limousine with Don on the way to Mt. Vernon and all the other sights on my wish list. He planned every minute of the weekend with me in mind. He was on a mission, and I felt like Cinderella going to the ball. As we arrived at different spots, there weren't many tourists around since it was winter. It was freezing cold, but the snow flurries felt good hitting my face. My favorite spot on the trip with my brother had been Woodlawn Plantation, and there I was years later driving right up to the front door, this time with Don and feeling like an invited guest instead of a tourist. The plantation was decorated for Christmas and looked like it was straight out of a Currier and Ives poster.

On the way back to DC, Don suggested we have lunch in Arlington, Virginia. As we walked down the main street lined with quaint little stores, he took my hand and led me into a charming little restaurant. My mind was racing with all sorts of thoughts. He was a friend. Was this more than a friendship? I was getting nervous again, but loving the attention and feeling like a princess.

As we returned to the hotel, Don said, "I'll meet you in the lobby in an hour, and we'll go on to the White House. I can only take one guest, so the others will meet us at The Kennedy Center."

I was a wreck getting dressed. Will I look OK? Is my dress right? Hair up? Hair down? It's been so long now, I don't even remember what I wore or what my hair looked like. What I do remember was walking out of the elevator, and there was Don, standing in front of the Christmas tree in his tux. He looked so handsome, and oddly enough, as he leaned over and kissed me on the cheek, it was how good he smelled that struck me. It was the same smell that sent me into orbit until the day he died.

We arrived at the West Portico of the White House. Back in those days, one didn't have to walk for blocks and go through the intricate screening like today. I had butterflies dancing in my stomach as we walked through the large double doors. *I must be dreaming. I'm in the White House for a party,* I thought.

This was December of 1997, and Bill Clinton was President. I marveled at the long hallway lined with a collage of recent photos of the president's family and events with world leaders. As we reached the end of the hall, and right on cue, a voice announced, "Mrs. Kathi Smith and Mr. Donald Koll." I think Don was enjoying watching my excitement more than he was being at the White House. He had been there many times before, but the fun he was having that night was watching and imagining through my eyes the joy of being there for the first time.

We walked up a long stairway that led to a small vestibule. As we turned the corner, there we were in the main entrance hall of the White House. The Marine Band, dressed in vibrant red jackets with shiny gold buttons, was playing glorious Christmas music. Guests were roaming through the White House rooms, drinks in hand. Christmas trees were lining the long hall connecting the East Room to the West Room with sparkling decorations throwing off glowing winks as they twinkled softly in the White House lights. A couple was standing next to me taking turns photographing one another. I quietly asked if they'd like me to take their picture together. They were so grateful—then I realized it was the actor Michael York and his wife, Pat.

It was all so surreal. We walked into one room and there was a life-size painting of George Washington looking down at us. President after president everywhere I turned. My favorite portrait, though, was the one of Jackie Kennedy. I had always admired her not only for the grace and intelligence she projected as First Lady but also for the independent spirit she showed throughout her life. She never talked or tried to defend herself. She was just right and didn't need anyone else's validation.

"Follow me," Don calmly said as we walked by the intricate gingerbread replica of the White House. "We're going to meet the president." A line was gathering, and Don knew not to linger but to get in place for the opportunity to be introduced. "Kathi, when you meet the president, say something he wants to hear so he'll talk to you. Otherwise you'll get a quick 'How do you do?' and that will be that." As I stood patiently in line, I couldn't help but think, *If the president talks to me then Don will be impressed.* It wasn't about the president; it was about Don.

We walked through doors so brilliantly varnished I could faintly see my reflection in them as we entered the Blue Room. There was the

President of the United States. The most powerful man in the world. My first thought was that he's much better-looking in person than on the television. He greeted us warmly, first shaking hands with Don then me. He didn't let go of my hand. He talked to me and looked into my eyes as if I was the only person in the world. Oh my. His charisma was incredible. I'd dare anyone—Republican or Democrat— not to have been completely charmed.

"Mr. President, my daughter has a friend at Stanford who knows your daughter, Chelsea, and I hear she's a wonderful girl." He politely thanked me, but I immediately figured out he had heard this line before. That little thought in the back of my mind kept reminding me that Don would be impressed if the president said more than two words to me. "Mr. President, I think we might have a friend in common." He was still holding my hand and now massaging my arm.

I'm sure Don was thinking, "Who in the world would she know that he would know?"

When I mentioned my friend's name, the president was surprised and said, "How do you know her?"

"How do you know her?" I quickly answered. I was questioning the president? I didn't mean to, but he was touching my arm, which made him seem like just a normal guy, not the President of the United States.

"I went all through grammar school with her," he said, "through high school with her. We were in carpool together. As a matter of fact, she was here for her birthday a couple of months ago."

"How do you spell her name?" It was a test because her name has an unusual spelling. I was thinking of anything to drag the conversation on, and it was working.

"L-E-Z-A-H," he immediately spelled.

"You do know her."

About that time, two men standing behind him motioned for us to move along. We did so, but the president didn't let go of my hand and stepped right in front of Don. He was trying to hide his "where does this guy think he's going?" face, but Don later told me he felt like punching him for flirting with his date but figured he'd be thrown in jail if he did so. One of the men put their hands on the president's shoulders and guided him back to his spot next to the Christmas tree.

"By the way," I said, looking back, "Lezah told me that 'Billy' told her he was going to be president one day."

"That's her story," he answered with a not-so-convincing smile on his face. "You've got to tell Hillary you know the Stingers."

The First Lady was watching all of this with a questioning expression. Don and I were introduced, and I mentioned our mutual friends. I noticing the surprised look on Don's and her faces and explained, "Well, many years ago I lived in Springfield, Missouri, where they live." I turned to the First Lady and added, "As a matter of fact, I recall you speaking at—"

"Stop, don't say any more," Mrs. Clinton said. "Were you at the Junior League when I spoke?" How could she have remembered that? It had been years.

Don and I walked out of the room, the doors closed, and we started laughing so hard we could barely stay standing. "If you can bullshit with the president," Don said, "you can bullshit with anyone."

We had arrived by limo, but apparently we were to leave by bus. "By bus? Like we're going to camp? Will we be singing '100 Bottles of Beer on the Wall'?" I teased.

"What kind of song is that? Kathi, don't start anything. There will be very important people on the bus—actors, supreme court justices, senators—"

"Don't worry," I laughed. "I won't start anything. I'm just having fun teasing you."

After the president paid tribute to each honoree with fun tidbits and stories of their accomplishments, he bestowed upon each one of them a large gold medallion hanging by a long ribbon of rainbow colors. The room broke out in applause, the Marine Band struck up more glorious music, and we strolled out of the White House caught up in the magic of the evening.

It was time for us all to get on the busses. The one we were escorted to was almost full, so we had to walk past all the "important people" to find a place in the back. As we walked down the aisle I spotted Bruce Springsteen.

"You're perfect." I couldn't help myself. I put my hand on his shoulder and said, "You can lead our camp songs." He immediately started singing "100 Bottles of Beer on the Wall." Don just shook his head in disbelief.

Arriving at The Kennedy Center was exciting in itself. As the busses rolled up, hundreds of people were waiting, vying to get a glimpse of who would appear. We followed the group down the Red Carpet with another crowd of fans lined up on both sides. No one paid any attention to us, but it was exciting to be a part of all the hoopla and enjoy our fifteen minutes of fame, as Andy Warhol would say.

The honorees that year were Charlton Heston, Lauren Bacall, Bob Dylan, Jessye Norman, and Edward Villella. Walter Cronkite was the Master of Ceremonies, and there were a slew of famous guests on stage introducing the performers paying special tribute to the honorees. Watching the president and First Lady take their places in the Presidential Box while "Hail to the Chief" played was magical. The show is recorded each year and televised around Christmastime, but there will never be one as exciting as that one—my first date with Don.

I didn't want the evening to end, and luckily we still had the dinner to go to.

We walked hand in hand into the foyer of The Kennedy Center, now filled with exquisitely decorated dining tables. The band was playing favorite musical pieces of each honoree, and some of them were even dancing on the small dance floor. Ladies in their gowns and men in their tuxes were sitting on the steps that led from the theater, just watching this illustrious group. The hall was filled with champagne toasts and laughter echoing from one end to the other.

We found our table, and to my utter surprise, I was seated next to Colin Powell. Vanessa Redgrave was seated on his other side. Some of the men at the table started quizzing him about his presidential aspirations, which was obviously a question he was not interested in engaging in. I overheard him mention India to Vanessa Redgrave and thought, *Ah ha. If Colin Powell talks to me, then Don will be impressed.* I had just been to India with my daughter Jennifer, so I easily became a part of their conversation.

Changing the subject on India, I said, "General Powell, correct me if I'm wrong, but didn't you dance with Princess Diana?" He seemed to be stunned I knew. She had just passed away a few months earlier, and a distinct sadness crossed his face.

"How did you know that? I don't think there were any pictures published."

"I think I read about it in *People Magazine*," I answered. "What was it like?"

"It was the day of my life." He looked me straight in the eyes as he recounted the deeply personal memory. "I received a phone call saying Princess Diana was being honored at an event and needed someone to dance with. I was chosen. I guess so-and-so was too short, another guy was out of the country, so for whatever reason, I was chosen. The day started with me sitting next to her at lunch. I mentioned I was going to dance with her that evening, which she seemed to be aware of. 'The problem,' I told her, 'is that I can't dance. I have two left feet and will probably step all over you.' Before I knew it, someone tapped me on the shoulder and asked me to follow them. I was led to a small room where the princess was standing with outstretched arms. She said, 'I think you need a dance class.' All of a sudden my left hand was locked into hers and my right hand was around her waist. She was saying, 'One to the left, two to the right, back step.' Princess Diana was teaching me how to dance. As she was walking out of the room, she mentioned, 'I probably ought to let you know that the dress I'm wearing tonight is backless, and when I say backless, I mean backless.' I asked what to do with my hand, and she looked back at me over her shoulder and said, 'That's for you to figure out.'"

"Amazing. What happened next?" I asked.

"Well, I was so nervous I went home and shot a few hoops in my driveway." Princess Diana had turned one of the most powerful men in the world into a fourteen-year-old marshmallow.

"Well, tell me more," I quizzed as I realized the entire table of twelve was listening to our one-on-one conversation. Even Don smiled at me, seeming to say, *Well, if she can bullshit with the president, she can bullshit with the general.* "Tell me about the evening. Did you dance with her?"

"I was so nervous that I realized my hands were cold," he laughed, "so I put them both between my knees and rubbed them together to warm them up."

"Oh no. Then what did you do?"

"Well, the only thing I could do. I wiped them off on the white tablecloth."

"Did you really dance with her alone in front of a room full of people?"

"I did."

"What did you do with your hand?"

"Right for the Royal Back," he answered, smiling ear to ear.

In a blink of time my trip was over. Cinderella was home, but in possession of both slippers, and just like Cinderella, I had a huge crush on the handsome prince.

Coming off of the DC weekend was an insurmountable task in itself. It was the beginning of a life that made me squint my eyes hard and wonder, *How was I so lucky?* It was a life most people dream of, and I was the fortunate girl to live it—both in good times and in bad.

Soon after our weekend in DC, my telephone rang (what a novel thought today, a phone call, not a text), and it was Don on the other end. "Kathi, I loved every minute of the weekend. Thank you for making it." He was thanking me? He had beaten me to the punch. Little old-fashion me had just sent him a handwritten thank-you note. He wasn't wasting any time. "How about visiting me in Aspen over Christmas vacation? I've been invited to a few fun parties and it would be great if you could join me."

I was so nervous he was asking me to once again go somewhere out of the neighborhood. "I'd love to," I said, "but my family will be with me over the holidays, and I really wouldn't feel comfortable leaving them." He understood, and we were both a little bummed I couldn't make it, but I felt it wouldn't be right to change my plans with my kids.

The day after Don's call was a rainy Sunday afternoon, and my son, Kevin, and I had decided to go to the latest James Bond movie. "Mr. Koll asked me to Washington, now Aspen; why can't he just ask me to a movie in our neighborhood?"

"Mom, why don't you just call him and see if he'd like to join us?"

"Are you kidding? I'm scared."

"No, Mom, you can do it. It's no big deal, just call him."

I took a deep breath and did it.

"Wow," I told Kevin. "That was pretty easy. He said yes. He's on his way."

Newport Beach was abuzz with Kathi & Don stories, Washington being the tipping of the scale. Our romance was probably a little slower than the town gossip, but that was OK. It was at our pace, and was fast enough for me to barely grasp. I was living in a world of emotions. I was going through a divorce, and at the same time, Don had come into my life. All sorts of emotions were hitting me like a hurricane.

We started having little dinners together, and that was when I truly learned how incredibly interesting Don was. He could talk about anything. It didn't matter if it was about local gossip, politics, history, or sports. He could engage in any subject, and with each topic I learned something new. He never pushed his beliefs on me or bragged, but he was educated and so versed on such a wide variety of topics.

Months went by as we enjoyed these little dinners. The most incredible aspect was his patience. We'd be at dinner, and out of nowhere, I'd burst out crying, "I can't believe I'm getting divorced. Patrick's a wonderful guy in so many ways. No one in my family has ever gotten divorced." He'd listen patiently and never pass judgment or try to sway me. He just listened. I'm not sure why he stuck in there, but he did and eventually the heavy emotional toll the divorce was taking on me lessened. I was falling in love with Don little by little, which was changing my world.

I'm not sure when the subject of marriage came up, but after a while, little hints were being thrown around about being together forever. We'd been a couple for less than a year, but as one of my friend's husbands said to me once, "Don's a real estate guy. When he sees what he wants, he goes for it and closes the deal." My friend had it right. I didn't see any reason to marry, but Don was of a different mindset. I asked him years later why it was so important to him. He had the same answer he did about our first date, "If I didn't marry you, someone else would."

Don's favorite place in the world, next to Cabo, was St. Tropez in Southern France. He had sold his boat, and rather than cruising around from port to port, he wanted to try living in a European town for a month. St. Tropez was the place he chose.

"Kathi, how about going to St. Tropez for the month of July?" How could I possibly turn that invitation down? I had been there a few times throughout the years since my first visit with my brother in 1976 and loved it. The only caveat was that I wanted my children to visit for part of our stay. I'd never been away from home that long and couldn't imagine being away from my family for a month. It was OK with Don, but first he wanted us to make an "advance run" to check out the house he had his eye on leasing.

It was May, and within the week, off we went. The trip wasn't meant to be long, but we planned a couple side trips along the way. When we reached St. Tropez, the wind was blowing, and the skies were threatening rain. We checked into the quaint Le Yaca Hotel in the old part of the village and after settling into our tiny, but very Provençal, room, we decided to go for a walk. It started to rain, and rain hard, but it didn't matter. We loved meandering through the streets and looking into shop windows, sharing one umbrella with nowhere in particular to go.

"Kathi, let's get back to the hotel and change out of our wet clothes. I have a spot picked out for dinner up in the hills." It had stopped raining but would soon be dark.

As we started to drive through the winding roads of Ramatuelle outside of St. Tropez, Don handed me a map and said, "You can be our navigator." The hotel concierge had recommended a restaurant in the hilltop village of Gassin. Finding it was an adventure unto itself, but a beautiful one. The damp trees and fields were glistening in the setting sun as we followed the winding roads toward our destination.

It was dark by the time we reached Gassin. The distant lights of St. Tropez could be seen miles beyond the rolling vineyard-laden hills as we walked towards the entrance to the village. There were only a few cobblestone streets and each were lined with little cottages covered in vines. I marveled how each entrance door was distinctive in its own way, exhibiting the pride of whoever lived there. At the end of the main street, there was a cluster of small restaurants. I took Don's lead as we walked hand in hand, over the stone walkway to his chosen spot. A red awning with the words *Le Micocoulier* was painted across the canvas, and a garden overlooking the valley below held a small cluster of tables and chairs, covered on account of the weather. As we walked through the entrance door and into the dining area, the maître d' greeted us warmly and showed us to a table by the window. He even seemed pleased with my attempt to use his language. The room was charming, with each table draped loosely by a Provençal tablecloth and lit softly by a flickering candle.

The salad had just been placed, and before I could even raise my fork to take a bite, Don was on one knee in front of me. I was wondering what he could possibly be doing. The restaurant was full of local people quietly dining, but at the same time, we were the only ones there.

"Kathi, I love you. Will you marry me?" From out of his pocket, he pulled the most beautiful ring I had ever seen.

"Yes."

We didn't notice that everyone was watching. One man stood up and announced, "She said 'Yes!'" There were cheers from the surrounding tables. All eyes had been on us, but our eyes had only been on each other.

When I went back years later, I could remember exactly where we sat. I had to see it one more time. I had to close that chapter of my life in order to move forward. I sat at the same little table and rubbed the tablecloth gently between my fingers, recounting each moment of that first dinner to my friend Laetitia. She had insisted on accompanying me on this last journey. Nothing had changed in this hilltop village or at *Le Micocoulier*. Laetitia sat across from me, and I described the evening as if it had been just yesterday. In some ways, it felt like it had been.

Don and I had been dating barely a year when one morning towards the end of December he called and asked if I'd like to have lunch with him. He didn't need to twist my arm, and within the hour, his car rolled up my driveway and I jumped in.

"So what's the occasion?" Dinner dates were now routine, but not lunch.

"I've been thinking 1/9/99 has a good ring to it. How about we get married that day?"

"Don, what are you talking about? That's ten days from now. How about 9/9/99? That has an even better ring to it."

"No way. We're on our way to Los Angeles to pick the spot."

"OK. I'm in, and I can't wait." There was no arguing with him, and I didn't want to.

I'm not sure whose idea it was, but somehow we both came to the conclusion of having a surprise wedding. We did tell our family, but swore them to secrecy. Other than family, we only invited friends who popped into our heads as people whom we had enjoyed being around during the last year. We were starting a new life together, and this made the most sense. We chose L'Orangerie, the most beautiful restaurant in Beverly Hills at the time. Sadly, it no longer exists, and I can't think of a more beautiful restaurant there today.

The manager, whom Don had called with a heads-up that we were coming, immediately met us as we walked through the doors of the restaurant. Once inside, one was transported into the most beautiful and romantic Parisian bistro this side of Paris—beautiful stone and slate floors, exquisite paneling graced with trompe-l'oeil, and an inner garden stealing any thoughts of a large metropolitan city outside. We had no need to look any further for the most romantic spot to start our life together surrounded by family and those friends who meant the most to us.

L'Orangerie was famous for a spectacular ten-foot-tall flower arrangement on top of the banquette dividing the room into two cozy sides. This would've posed a problem for anyone other than Don, since we wanted everyone together. He offered to send in a crew of carpenters to remove it, promising to have it all replaced by lunch the day following our wedding.

There were two things I was certain about: my love for Don and not wanting any stress. We picked the menu right then and there and decided to use the florist who already worked in that space. Instead of formal invitations, we called friends for a dinner party. I gave myself one day to find a dress, and when I didn't find anything I liked as much as something I already had, I gave up looking.

We came up with a list of 120 people, which was the maximum capacity for the restaurant. With each phone call I made, I simply said, "Hi *so-and-so*, Don and I are having a small dinner party for eight to ten people on January ninth and would love for you to join us. And by the way, please don't mention this to anyone. We don't want to hurt anyone's feelings."

The evening was upon us. Everything was in its place—the banquette removed, spectacular topiary flower arrangements on each table, ivy-draped chandeliers hanging in the inner garden, which had been transformed into a dance floor, and seating cards lined up by the entrance. As our guests arrived one after another, and it quickly became obvious that we weren't having a dinner for eight to ten friends. There was a buzz circulating that we were going to announce our engagement. Apparently there were a number of bets going on, too. When one friend said to another that she guessed we were getting married, the other woman said, "No way, I've seen Kathi in that dress before. She'd never get married in an old dress."

There was a definite excitement in the air with our little bit of mystery giving everyone something to chat about. Don and I made a point to move quickly through the room greeting everyone before too many questions were asked.

"Let's go," Don said, leading me to a small platform where the musicians were playing.

The music stopped, and everyone gathered to hear what looked to be a toast from Don. With a sparkle in his eyes, he lifted his glass of champagne and said, "Thank you all for coming tonight. We were going to have a Christmas party, but time got away from us. Then we thought we'd have a New Year's Eve party but found out many of you would be out of town. So we thought, why not have a Wedding party. We'd like for you all to meet Superior Court Judge Paul Flynn."

The doors opened and in walked the judge. As he made his way through the crowd, it was as if the Red Sea were parting. There was stunned silence. Onto the little stage he leapt, and right then and there we were married. The cheers, applause, and whistles could probably be heard for miles. We had succeeded in surprising all 120 people.

* * *

While our life together was just starting, we knew our little family wasn't finished growing. Nothing makes a house feel like a home more than a dog, and ours wouldn't be complete without our yellow lab, Abby.

"Kathi," Don called me from his office early one morning, "what are you doing right now?"

"Is something wrong?"

"No, something is fantastic. Meet me at the airport. I think I've found the perfect dog for us." He had the enthusiasm of Christmas morning when a kid gets his first red Schwinn bicycle.

"What? We're taking a plane to get a dog? What in the heck are you talking about?" I asked.

"It's a surprise. Meet me in thirty minutes. We have to hurry."

We had just lost my Tibetan terrier, Mollie, a "white, fluffy dog" as Don described her. "Kathi, I like your dog, but she's not a dog. She's a little white fluffy thing. A real dog is a male Lab or a Retriever." Don had always had big dogs and made me promise our next dog would be a "real dog."

I hurried to the airport, and within minutes, we were off. I always loved his spontaneity, and we were always game for whatever life brought us. After we settled onto the plane, we breathed a sigh of relief that we had made it.

"I got a call this morning from a friend who told me an old buddy of mine from Cub Scout days recently died," Don shared. "Apparently my old friend had been involved for years with an organization that trained and provided guide dogs to the blind, but he had never asked for a dog. Before he passed, he made it clear he wanted me to have one of the dogs who hadn't passed the final test to move on to live with a blind person."

"But Don. I want a puppy to bond with," I cried.

"I don't want to struggle with the puppy years. Trust me, we'll bond," he promised. "We'll never leave the dog out of our sight for the next thirty days. One of us will be with it constantly, 24/7."

I knew nothing about guide dogs when we spent the day at the Guide Dogs for the Blind campus in San Rafael, California. It's a beautiful eleven-acre spot nestled in a park-like environment and houses around three hundred dogs. We were greeted warmly and taken on a tour of the facility. Our tour guide was a lovely young woman who had a lot of enthusiasm for the program. She brought along a German Shepard to demonstrate the high level of training the dogs acquire. We walked all over the campus, visiting the veterinarian hospital, the kennels, and the apartments where recipients live while they are being trained with their dogs. It was incredible.

I could hardly keep up with our guide as she quickly led us in and out of rooms, down trails, over fields. All of a sudden it clicked with me—I think the sunglasses gave her away, certainly not the ease in which she and her trusted dog moved. "Are you blind?" I nervously asked.

"Yes," she answered. "I've been 100% blind since I was thirty-five years old due to an accident."

Don and I were stunned. What an inspiration she was. Her enthusiasm and zest for life as well as the love between her and her dog was incredible. Her dog was her vision, and it took me an hour to realize she was blind. I was astounded.

We were led into a small office where we waited patiently to meet the dog they had matched with the paperwork Don had filled out. There were many questions about our lifestyle, our experience with dogs, our desire to care for such a highly trained animal, and general inquiries into what kind of people we were. The organization takes great pride in matching dogs not only with the right blind recipient, but also with those who are given the opportunity to care for a retired guide dog or a dog who is unable to move on to actual guiding. "Flunked" is hardly the correct word; "Career Changed" is a better description of those dogs who don't pass the stringent testing for all sorts of different reasons.

In walked Corsica, a stately yellow Labrador making a career change due to a persistent ear infection, a condition which a blind person wouldn't be able to spot. She was probably the most beautiful and well-trained dog I had ever met. We looked at her with amazement and were instantly drawn to her dark chestnut eyes circled with what looked like eye makeup. I was ready to scoop her up in an instant, but reluctantly said, "Do you have any available male dogs?" I think they were surprised, but said yes and asked us to come back after lunch for introductions.

"They handed us the perfect dog. What's wrong with you?" He never had to raise his voice. Just the way he said things sometimes gave me butterflies in my stomach. I always called it his "strong side." Years later, the nurses knew exactly what I meant.

"Don, I did it for you. You have always told me you've only had male dogs and never wanted a female one, remember? If you're alright with a girl, let's go back and see if they'll give her to us." Leaving my uneaten lunch on the table, we darted out of the restaurant, nervous that another couple would be gifted her before we got back to the center.

"We have two male dogs to introduce you to," said the director. They were led in one by one. Strong, beautiful, huge yellow Labs. But Corsica peeked around the door. We were in love. I would like to think she was too.

"Can she fetch?" I asked her trainer before we left.

"Uh, well, the people who need guide dogs don't normally play fetch with them, but you can teach her," he said and gave me a few training tips. I felt so silly for even asking.

With that, we had found our baby. And as we walked out the door with her, who would have ever guessed that this Career Changed guide dog would have an incredible service job in her future. Life sometimes works in strange ways, or should I say miracles.

The first thing we did was change her name. Don and I couldn't imagine saying, "Here, Corsica. Sit, Corsica. Down, Corsica." We settled on Abby. I don't know why, but it just seemed to fit her. We bonded just as Don had promised. And as he insisted, she was never without one of us for the first thirty days. If she couldn't come with us, we stayed home. If a restaurant didn't allow her in, we'd order takeout and eat on the sidewalk. We made it work.

One evening we decided to walk to our favorite local restaurant, where we thought she'd be allowed on the patio. Alas, we ended up ordering takeout and sitting out front. Various friends stopped to ask what we were doing as they filtered into the restaurant, which gave us the perfect opportunity to introduce Abby and explain our situation. Next thing we knew, wine was being delivered to us in paper cups. There we were, eating pasta and illegally drinking on a public sidewalk. Abby had her first job—guiding us home.

Abby and Don

Abby has been the thread of compassion, unconditional love, and unwavering devotion in our lives. She has served as the breathing life lesson of how a dog can bring pleasure to someone disabled and at the same time teach a gentle, caring way of love to my grandchildren.

No matter how sad I've been, she's always been there with her big brown, dreamy eyes looking at me and her gentle little kisses licking my hands. She almost never left Don's side, and if he wasn't looking at me, he was looking at her.

It's always been easy to know how Abby is feeling. A smile and wagging tail when I'm home lifts my spirits, but such a sad face at the window watching me drive away puts a little pep in my step to get home. She even sits under my feet no matter where I am in the house and sleeps on the floor next to me, just as she did for Don.

3

MR. AND MRS. KOLL GO TO WASHINGTON

"Adventure is worthwhile in itself."
—Amelia Earhart

There are certain times in one's life that will never be forgotten for many reasons, and July of 2001 just happened to be one of those. We were in our dream vacation spot: *Le Patio* in Les Parcs de St. Tropez. It was the paradise where we spent the most concentrated time, and the villa we rented each year felt like home in so many ways.

Don and I had been invited to a dinner party in Cap d'Antibes, France. It was unusual for Don to say yes to venturing very far from St. Tropez, but he thought it sounded fun and said, "Go ahead and accept." The day of the dinner threatened rain, and Don's mood soured at the idea of driving to Cap d'Antibes in bad weather. "Get us out of it," he said.

I said, "Don, if you had said this to me a few days ago, I could have come up with an excuse, but it's too late now. We can't be rude and cancel the day of. Let's just leave early and make an adventure of it."

We had bought a new Porsche that summer in Stuttgart, Germany, which we had tucked away in the St. Tropez garage to be shipped back to the States at the end of our vacation. We didn't use it much, especially with the reputation of crime in Southern France.

On this particular morning, our houseguests had our rental car, so we thought it would be fun to put a few miles on the almost empty odometer driving along the Côte d'Azur in our silver turbocharged Porsche.

As we packed the car with our dinner clothes, Don was still complaining about leaving until I said, "Come on, Don. You always say, 'You can't worry about things you can't change.' We're committed; let's just have fun."

"OK, but don't talk me into this again," he said gruffly. "Next time they come to us."

Off we went, waving to the staff as we drove up the cobblestone driveway from *Le Patio*. Once out the front gates, we followed the winding road lined with pink oleanders, each French home we passed more charming than the next. We passed through the guard gate, waved to our friendly neighborhood guard, and we were off. I always marveled at how Don could maneuver the narrow streets of the old town of St. Tropez. The village was within minutes of our house and always our exit route, no matter how much traffic there was or what direction we were really going. We just had to drive through the town. We passed the first place I stayed at in 1976 with my brother Don, the Hotel Le Yaca, and the Sénéquier where Don spent countless hours as I combed the local shops with friends. We passed the boats, each one larger than the next, and street artists we were on a first name basis with.

Once out of town, our adventure began. As we drove through the forest towards the highway, the sky opened up, and it began to pour. Don pulled over in front of a roadside convenience store. "Let's go in and wait for the storm to pass." We weren't there for very long when he said under his breath, "Let's go."

"Why?" I countered. "It's still pouring out there." He motioned towards a man in the corner who I had also noticed. He seemed to be staring at us, and we agreed there was something unsettling about him. We got absolutely soaked just running the short distance to our car. We drove off, but it was raining so hard we couldn't see five feet in front of us, so Don pulled over under an overpass where we stayed close to an hour. We didn't dwell on the guy in the store, but we agreed how creepy it was that he seemed to watch our every move while talking on a mobile phone. Don was always very aware of his surroundings after taking a kidnapping avoidance class while officing in Mexico City, and he felt that the whole situation seemed unnerving. I was inclined to agree.

The clouds parted, and we were enjoying the bright, sunny Côte d'Azur as we sped along the highway. I couldn't help but secretly feel like I was Grace Kelly and he was Cary Grant in *To Catch a Thief*. Don, handsome and tanned, me feeling the breeze off the sea and through my hair. We were creating new memories and a history together rich with meaning and happiness. Don made me feel as if my life with him was like living in a movie, a dream, an adventure unlike any other. Like two little kids always raring to go, living life with a zest unmatched. I didn't think it was possible to be so happy or so in love.

It was approaching noon when we reached Villefranche-sur-Mer, a charming historic seaport village on the Mediterranean Sea. Don had his favorite restaurant on the port where we took time to savor our *déjeuner, notre vin, et l'atmosphere*. Next to St. Tropez, Villefranche is my favorite village in Southern France. The old part along the water has a beautiful bay perfect for idling the day away at lunch while watching magnificent boats with anchors dropped and passersby diving into the refreshing water of the Med before a hike along the shore or a walk into town. The cobblestone streets and narrow passageways are rich with history dating back hundreds of years.

After lunch, we had time to kill before arriving at our friends' home, and I suggested we check out *Institut de Français*, a total-immersion

French school I had been contemplating applying to. The school was located high above the village on the side of the hill, with an incredible view overlooking charming rooftops and the sea. We rang the bell and were immediately welcomed with enthusiasm by the secretary in the front office. She gave us a wonderful tour, but as we were about to leave, it took a rather strange turn. "Where did you park your car? You should be very careful around here. The summer months are full of gypsies looking for unsuspecting tourists. Always be aware of your surroundings."

Don and Kathi in Villefranche-sur-Mer

We meandered down the winding street from the school, actually taking a wrong turn and ending up at the seaport again. Without a care in the world and no timeframe, we both laughed and agreed that there was no better adventure in the world than finding our way through villages of France. Within minutes we were back on track on the lower Corniche with its narrow two-lane road hugging the hillside above the Sea. Don pulled over at a small lookout point and said, "Jump out. Let's get a good photo of the town." There was only enough room for one car, and the space between my door and the small cliff wall was only a couple of feet. I left my door open and stood looking at the magical view below. Don quickly got out and was standing next to me. "Take a picture," he said.

I was looking through the lens of the camera, waiting for the clouds to part for that perfect awe-inspiring photo when I heard Don yelling words I'd never heard him say. He was screaming, swearing—his voice was strong with incredible confidence, but in those few seconds I was completely confused about what in the world was happening. I looked towards the car, and there in my seat was Don. I leaned in and realized there was a stranger in the driver's seat.

Don was hunched over the stick shift, pulling up on the brake with one hand and striking this stranger with the other with all his might. He had his head in the guy's ribcage and was trying to poke at his eyes with his index and middle finger. Neither of us would have done what we did if we had stopped to think, but instinct and adrenaline drove us into action. Seconds seemed to move in slow motion, and I can still remember each one clearly. I dove on top of Don as he continued to struggle. Up went the hand brake by Don; down went the brake by the intruder. The car was screaming. The robber mistakenly put the car into third gear, which resulted in jerky leaps and bounds rather than smoothly racing off as was his intention. My face was within inches of the guy. He had dark skin, wraparound sunglasses, and was, much to my surprise, rather handsome. (How in the world did I notice that?) "Leave us alone," I yelled. "Leave us alone!" The car took a leap, and I was thrown out onto the pavement. I got up and immediately jumped back into the fray. The three of us were now committed, and there was no turning back. *I'm going to be killed, but I've got to help Don*, I thought through the panic. The car continued screaming as it was over-revved again and again.

Again I was face-to-face with this wretched man. Once more I yelled. I screamed, but his conviction was not lost on our aggressive self-defense. *He can't win*, I kept thinking. *He can't hurt us. This isn't happening.*

My small Elph Canon camera was still dangling from my wrist, and without a bit of hesitation, I raised my hand and as quickly and as hard as possible I swung the metal camera towards him. I made contact. A direct hit to his face. His glasses shattering into a thousand pieces, head turning left and right as he arched his back, knuckles tightening on the steering wheel as they turned white. I started to back away when the car took another leap, but this time my tee shirt caught the side of the door, which grabbed me as the car jumped ahead. I was flung into the air and came down through the glass and hit the top of the door so hard I felt my breath get knocked out of me. I landed in a pile of glass with my head snug against the door; I saw blood smudged along the side of the car. I thought it must be my blood, but I felt OK. If the car was put into reverse, I would be run over, dragged, and killed. I was completely vulnerable and curled into a fetal position. Helpless.

The car took off. The door slammed shut with Don inside. I attempted to get up, each movement cutting me more and more. People appeared from all directions and were trying to comfort me. They could only speak a few furtive words of English. "Kidnap," I yelled. "Kidnap!" Between Don's kidnap avoidance lessons, the strange man in the convenience store, and the harrowing experience I was having, my initial thought was that he had been kidnapped. The car was completely out of view, and I stood there thinking how fast everything had happened, how I had found the love of my life and how suddenly he was gone. I kept thinking about how much I loved him and he was gone. What was happening? Strangers were telling me to sit down and directed me to a small wall where we had been standing, with a five-hundred-foot drop to the sea. Another woman grabbed me by my shirt and said, "No, she's in shock. She can't sit here; she will fall."

The ambulance and police arrived. People were crying. One man said in his best but broken English, "I wanted to help, but I didn't know who the bad guy was." I noticed that there were no more cars coming towards us. My heart sank. I knew the only thing that could have happened was that they had gone off the cliff.

Later, Don told me he had grabbed the steering wheel and turned the car into the oncoming traffic. He knew it was his only chance of survival. The car stopped, and the guy jumped out. He started to run, but turned and tried to pull my beach bag from the back seat. It was a struggle for him because the front seat was locked into position and there wasn't enough room to squeeze the bag through the small opening. I had no idea the bag was there. Don had had a funny feeling we would be robbed that summer, so he took my jewelry from our safe and brought it with us in this little canvas bag. Don leaned over, pulled back his arm and then let go with a hard right hook right into the guy's jaw—possibly breaking it. He went flying. When he picked himself up off the ground, he hopped into a blue Mercedes, which had apparently been trailing us. Our little Porsche sat in the middle of the road looking quite abused and barely drivable, but some onlookers came to Don's aid.

In the distance, through my tears I could make out three figures walking in the middle of the road towards this little crowd of people trying to help me. It was Don. He had a woman on either side walking with him. Their arms were holding him up as he emotionally took one look at me, and noticing the blood on my shirt, started to cry. We fell into one another's arms with relief and shock.

The medics wanted to take me to the hospital, but Don looked me over and said, "Come on, Kathi, they're superficial wounds. You're OK, and if we go to the hospital, we'll be there all day." Once again,

Don was the eternal optimist, and we were on to another adventure without ever looking back.

We thought we escaped everything with the carjacking, but a week later things changed. It started out as a day like all the rest. Don and I jumped into the speedboat we rented each summer and headed for town where he liked to sit at a little cafe sipping his coffee and watching the morning activity of the port. I usually sat with him for a few minutes then walked around the village looking in the windows of all the charming little shops. By 10:00 AM, we would scurry back to the house and grab our things before heading to the beach, which Don always expected us to do by boat. He loved driving the boat; it was an exact model of the one he had at home in Newport. As soon as we passed through the speed control area, he would put the throttles forward and speed over the waves. "I have the need for speed," he'd say, quoting his favorite expression from *Top Gun*. We'd fly over the waves, passing sailboats and leaving everyone in our wake.

But that day, the young man who helped with the boat said there was something wrong with its engine, and he'd have to take the boat to the mechanic. While we were getting ready, he said Mario, the chef, had asked him for a quick ride to a beach cove because he was taking the day off. When he did, he noticed a strange noise and thought it best we didn't take the boat out into the open sea until it could be checked.

Pascal, the guardian of the house, said he'd give us a ride by car to the beach and pick us up when we were ready. I can't for the life of me remember why we didn't just drive ourselves, but we took him up on it.

As we were leaving, I noticed that the maid Anna was cleaning behind the books on the shelf outside our room. I passingly thought, *That's strange; most of the time one has to ask a maid to be so thorough.* She was new this summer and seemed out of place. She was from

Poland—tall, beautiful, more like a model than a maid. I didn't have a good feeling about her, though; her demeanor was strange. When she casually asked if we knew anything about a painting hanging in the bedroom, I thought it was a weird question. It was hard to put my finger on my feelings, but I felt uncomfortable around her.

After our usual day of swimming, beach, and lunch at Le Club 55, we were ready to go home. Pascal was in the parking lot waiting for us. All the way home, he talked about all the work he had done in the garden, and when we got home, he insisted on showing us the lawn down the hill he had mowed. *Why was he making such a big deal about where he mowed the lawn?* I wondered.

The house was void of the usual afternoon activity since the staff had the day off. A couple of them returned, but went to their rooms. It was actually a nice respite. I sometimes thought of our July visit to *Le Patio* like a summer stock play. All the drama of so many personalities, the month of bonding with everyone and then POOF—the "play" quickly comes to a close at the end of July. Not to reopen until the following summer.

While I puttered around the quiet house, Don sat in his usual after-beach spot on the patio overlooking the Med, snacking on peanuts and a Diet Coke while reading a book and watching the boats speeding back to the port from the beaches. We were invited to dinner that evening at our friends' Heidi and Alberto's home, and Don decided to take a nap while I started getting ready.

I walked in and said, "Why are there papers all over the floor?"

"The shutters were left open, and a wind must have come in." Don was not nearly as concerned as I was.

I thought something looked different when I opened the closet, but couldn't place my finger on it for a moment. "The safe is gone," I gasped.

"What do you mean?" he said, jumping out of bed and passing me in the little vestibule, looking at the missing spot in my closet where the safe had been. He got on a chair and looked above the doorframe into a small crevice. "Son of bitch—the money's gone."

"What do you mean?" I had no idea what he was talking about. "What money?"

"I've hidden cash here all these years," he said, "to pay the staff for incidentals and tips."

Mario and Pascal appeared at our doorway with a look of horror on their faces. They held our American flag, which they found on the ground at the foot of the steps to the dock. We were upset over the robbery, but also fearful of what the symbol of our flag being torn down meant. The first year we rented the house, we had asked our neighbors if they felt comfortable with us flying an American flag at an old lookout tower on the property lined up across the bay from the ancient fort in town, and no one had any complaints. The flag had served two purposes: to display patriotism to our country and to let everyone know we were back in town. Seeing our flag in pieces brought tears to both of us. One day, we were awakened early in the morning with music of "The Star-Spangled Banner" blaring. Don and I jumped out of bed and stood on the little porch outside our room in our white terry cloth robes, witnessing a US naval ship passing by. All hands on deck saluting the flag. Now we were staring at that very same beloved flag in tatters.

The police were called and arrived quickly. They began questioning the household over and over again. I listened intently and learned a few things I had not known. The maid from the previous year was still Pascal's girlfriend and had two brothers who had recently been released from jail for robbery. Anna, the Polish maid, also had a boyfriend just released from jail for robbery. What a wonderful group we were dealing with. Of course when questioned, everyone had an alibi. The chef was at the beach. The maid was let off early. The boat captain was with the boat at the mechanic's. Pascal was outside mowing the lawn.

I telephoned our friends to beg off dinner, but Heidi said, "You have to come. Everyone wants to see you and Don to try to cheer you up. You can't just stay home and be sad." It was rather sweet to hear coming from a household of Europeans. We had made true friends during our summers, and they wanted to embrace us—and of course hear all the gossip. We finally got there and did end up at having a nice evening.

The next morning, a friend from New York called. He had heard the story. As a matter of fact, the story was spreading like wildfire with great exaggeration with respect to the value of the jewels. The numbers became so exaggerated that Don considered hiring a bodyguard for us or guard dogs for the house. I, the girl in shorts and tee shirts, now had the ridiculous reputation of having a jewelry collection fit for royalty. Everyone was talking about things I never owned, couldn't afford, and if I did, would not be stupid enough to bring on a summer vacation. The story took on a life of its own.

The last ten days of our vacation were completely wrapped up with solving the mystery of the robbery and carjacking. We went to the police station with Laetilia, owner of Le Yaca Hotel, who had become a good friend and volunteered to help with translation. Don was certain it was an inside job. The police immediately took Pascal to the police station, where they put him in jail, but after three days, they didn't feel they had enough evidence to keep him any longer.

As our monthlong vacation neared the end, I announced to Don that I never wanted to be in that house again. A few days later, I looked outside and spotted him on the veranda in a rather intense conversation with a woman I'd never seen before. "Who was that?" I asked when she left.

"She was the owner's secretary," he said with a broad smile. "I just made an offer on the house."

"What?" I said. "Weren't you listening to me earlier? I don't ever want to step foot into this place again. Why would you make an offer on it?"

"It's the perfect time," he said. "The reputation of the robbery is bringing down the home's value, and it will be a great investment." That was Don, ever the real estate guy. Much to his chagrin, the owner would never sell that place, robbery or no.

Our last day was bittersweet. We had spent so many wonderful times there over the years with family and friends. I think our hearts were really in the place, but after all the drama, I was ready to move on to another spot and make new memories. Hopefully ones without danger and drama. Before leaving the house for the last time, Don stood on the little chair and looked into his hiding spot one more time. "Son of a gun," I heard him yell. "The money's back."

Driving up the driveway, we waved goodbye to the staff for what we thought was our last time. On the way to the airport, we relived each moment. Don felt both the carjacking and house robbery were connected inside jobs. He also believed that the staff probably split the money from the sale of the jewelry, but whoever had the cut in his cash above the door felt guilty or scared and returned it. I guess I'll never know, but Don convinced me to go back. Kind of like getting back on a horse again, and we had many more wonderful years there—minus the drama that is now part of the folklore of the village.

On the homefront, there was more excitement in store. Luckily for us, though, it was excitement of a different kind. I've had an interest in politics since a rainy day in 1976 when, at the young age of twenty-five, I was chosen at the local courthouse in Springfield, Missouri, to be a state delegate representing Ronald Reagan for President.

He didn't win that year, but the excitement for the process of the caucus and of the campaign were contagious.

Don had been involved with the elections of former Presidents Nixon, Reagan, Bush 41, and Bush 43. He actually built President Nixon's Presidential Library and, along with two other friends, bought The Western White House from him when President Nixon decided to leave California. From lively dinner discussions about who should be the next president to an emotional visit from Nancy Reagan shortly after her husband's death, Don's stories of times spent with former presidents are fascinating and could fill their own book.

During the 2000 campaign of former President George W. Bush, I surprised Don one day by saying, "Guess who's coming for dinner next week."

He was pretty shocked when my answer was Laura Bush.

"Wow, Kathi," he said. "Good for you."

Don, Laura Bush, and Kathi

I had offered to do a small fundraising dinner in her honor, and to my delight, I received a call from Jack Oliver, who at the time served as the national finance director for then-Governor Bush's presidential election, giving me the green light. The dinner was in our garden in Beverly Hills for twenty guests and turned out to be one of those magical California evenings we all pray for. Perfect weather, clear skies with a view beyond the towers of Century City to the Pacific Ocean, along with a breathtaking sunset of bright oranges and pinks silhouetting the mountain range across the canyon from our home. All of this as the first course was being served. The date was September 13, 2000.

As Mrs. Bush was leaving my home she said, "What a beautiful evening this was. If I'm lucky enough to move into the White House, it will be my turn to entertain you. Please do let me know if you're ever in DC."

Soon after winning the election, President Bush appointed me to the Board of Trustees of The John F. Kennedy Center for the Performing Arts, which meant I was going to be in Washington on a regular basis.

Within a few months, I was in DC for my first Kennedy Center meeting and decided to take Mrs. Bush up on her offer. I called the White House and left word with her assistant that Don and I were in town and would love to see her. Word came back that she'd love to see Don the next time, but she was hosting a small ladies' luncheon in honor of the Queen of Thailand, and she would be delighted for me to attend. And if I could make it, would I please come early so we'd have a chance to visit.

I was a wreck choosing what to wear.

I was directed to enter the White House by way of the long driveway winding through the South Lawn. My heart was racing. I had absolutely no idea what to expect. I was escorted into the Diplomatic Receiving Room where I was then taken to an elevator that carried me to a small vestibule outside the living quarters.

I wasn't sure what to do when the doors opened. The gentleman who had operated the elevator through many administrations said, "Go ahead. You're invited, aren't you? Just walk up to the door."

The door was ajar a bit. I wasn't sure whether I should knock, walk in, or just say, "Yoo-hoo, I'm here." All of a sudden the door opened and there was Mrs. Bush. I'm sure she sensed my nervousness. With perfect decorum, she immediately put me at ease by giving me a hug and then a little tour as we waited for the other guests to arrive. "Kathi," she asked, "how do you like the tiger print fabric I've put on this small sofa? My mother-in-law can't believe I chose it."

"She got to decorate the way she wanted when she lived here," I said with a sly grin. "It's your turn now, and I think it's fabulous."

The other guests, including Condoleezza Rice, started arriving. When it was time to be seated, I thought there might be a mistake on the seating chart. I decided to wait till everyone else was seated to find the one empty seat left. There I was, next to Condoleezza Rice and one seat away from Mrs. Bush. I've never been one for "ladies' luncheons," but this one was one I could have repeated. The White House. The Guests. Me. What in the world was I doing there?

I wanted the afternoon to last forever, but as the saying goes, "All good things must come to an end." Mrs. Bush walked with us into the vestibule to say good-bye. As I stepped into the elevator my heel wedged down into the track making it impossible for the door to close or for any of us, including Condoleezza Rice and the Queen's assistant, to leave. I subtlety tried to pull my shoe out, but to no avail. I'm sure not more than a minute passed by, but the silence, the looks and my imagining the White House engineer arriving to pull my shoe out of the track was giving me true anxiety. I quickly slipped my bare foot out of my shoe, got on my knees and pulled my heel out of the track. Mrs. Bush was smiling as the door closed. The other ladies were looking at me in silence.

"Whew, do you know what a close call that was?" I said. "The President almost had to go door to door all over Washington to see whose foot would fit into this shoe." The silence was broken and everyone started laughing.

I was fortunate that Mrs. Bush invited me to join her in the private quarters a number of times, including once with just her and her mother. Each time I would receive an invitation, Don would remind me how involved he had been throughout the years with former presidents and had never been invited to the private quarters. "Don't worry. I get it; I'm working on it," I told him.

In October of 2005, I was once again in DC for a Kennedy Center meeting. Don was home in California. I called Mrs. Bush's office when I arrived to see if she could meet me at a restaurant for lunch the following day. Word came back she'd love to get together, but would it be OK if I came to The White House? It would be less complicated for her. Since it had been my invitation, and I looked at it as if I were the hostess, I took a stab with a little white lie, and said, "That would be great, but Don's joining us, so I hope it's OK if he comes too."

Word came back, "Mrs. Bush would love to see Don."

"Don," I quickly called home, "get on a Red Eye. You're in for lunch at The White House tomorrow."

He arrived early the next morning raring to go. I loved being the one with experience this time as we approached 1600 Pennsylvania Avenue. "Don, first we're going to go into The Diplomatic Receiving Room. Follow me, Don. The elevator is over here, and Mrs. Bush will be waiting for us when we walk into a small vestibule." I was driving him crazy, but I also knew he was loving every moment of it and getting a kick out of me.

"Did I happen to mention I invited the President too?"

"What?" He said with unquestionable shock in his voice. "How could you invite the President of the United States to lunch at the White House?"

"Well, the way I look at it, I'm the hostess, and what's there to lose? I was only being nice asking. And who knows, maybe he's like the prom queen who no one ever asks out, and he's just going to be having a peanut butter and jelly sandwich at his desk. All he has to say is no."

We stepped out from the elevator, and right on cue, Mrs. Bush was waiting to greet us. Her warmth and easy manner immediately made us feel welcomed, and within minutes she made us feel like she was the lucky one to have us.

The President arrived. He said he was so happy we got word to him that we were going to be there. I quickly glanced over at Don, eyebrows raised with a wide-eyed smile. We followed the two of them to the small sitting area under the famous arched window that looks towards The Old Senate Building. The conversation flowed easily from trivia to politics to the President saying, "Prince Charles is coming next week and I'm going to be seated next to Camilla. What in the heck am I going to talk to her about?"

"Don can coach you," I quickly answered. "He's been seated next to her a number of times and has really enjoyed her."

The President looked at me and said, "How is it that you two have been hanging around them?" I shrugged my shoulders, looked around the room and with a big smile replied,

"Well, look where we are today, who would have guessed"

"You have a point there," he said, shaking his head and laughing.

4

THE DAY MY WORLD STOOD STILL

*"Rock bottom became the solid foundation
in which I rebuilt my life."*
—J. K. Rowling

October 27, 2005—the day that changed everything. The peak of the mountain—or was it the bottom of the sea? I had two lives with Don, and this day was the dividing line.

Every moment of that day is etched into my memory, starting with waking up in Don's arms. We had a habit of sleeping nose to nose with my leg wrapped around him, like two pieces of a puzzle never to be separated. He slowly started kissing me, distracting me from my scheduled appointment with the subcontractors I was about to meet but quickly forgot. It was a way we started many mornings, but this one wasn't like others. I distinctly remember thinking at the time that something was really different. What was it?

Our lovemaking had always been as good as my imagination could take me, but *this* morning was special. It was better than I could ever possibly imagine. It wasn't the mechanics; it was something much more. Every nerve in my body felt completely loved. I didn't want it to ever end. Life couldn't be this good. How could I be this happy? Feel so in love? As we quietly rested in one another's arms, I glanced out the window and spotted a boat cruising by. The early morning light on the bay sparkled through our partially opened blinds, and I could hear the soft sounds of seagulls in the distance. My thoughts drifted to how ideal my life truly was. I didn't want the moment to pass, but true to form, Don sprang up and was ready to get on with his day.

Whether or not the housekeeper was coming, our normal routine was to make our bed together. This was Don's habit, probably starting with his prep school days at Harvard Military School where, as a Prefect in charge of younger classmates, he always won the prize for best-kept dorm room. The teachers didn't know his room was merely a "set." He found a shed behind the school where he convinced his classmates to "keep their shit" so their room always looked perfect. Those early days instilled in him an unbreakable habit of beginning the day with a perfectly made bed. We actually had fun standing across from each other and taunting one another about whose side looked better or who could finish faster.

Over a breakfast of scrambled eggs, I reminded Don that we were meeting the contractor next door to start remodeling the home we had recently purchased. I waited patiently while Don read the paper before I brought up a few remodeling questions. Originally when buying the house, Don's intention was to tear it down and build something new. Normally I would have loved that idea, but this home was built in 1927 and had an impossible-to-replace uniqueness. We had agreed that we would do some minor changes, live in it for a year, and then decide to keep it or scrap it. I secretly felt that that was Don's idea of quieting me down and during that year he'd slowly work me over with new house plans. Knowing this was in the back of his mind, I figured he'd be conservative on some of the remodeling decisions. I wanted this to be a fun experience for both of us, so I said slyly, "Don, can you just say yes?"

"What do you mean, Kathi?" I wasn't asking with the intention of taking advantage of him, but I didn't want us to start out bickering over little things like cabinet knobs.

"Please just say *yes*." OK, I admit, I sounded like a little girl.

"Go next door while I finish the paper," he said, ignoring my pleas. "I'll do the dishes and meet you in twenty minutes." Obviously he just wanted to finish reading without listening to my chatter, and the dishes were a small price to pay.

I met the team upstairs in what was to be our new master bedroom. It was long and narrow, and it was closer to the bay than most homes along the strip because it was built before the city setback rules. With windows on three sides, the view was unobstructed and gave the feeling of perpetually living on a boat. The carpet had already been pulled up, and the guys were eager to get started. All of a sudden, I heard the front door fling open and the sound of Don running up the wooden stairs. He burst into our room, all energy and enthusiasm. After shaking hands with the men, he picked up a hammer and threw it into the wall. "It's my tradition when starting a new home," he explained with a broad smile in response to the contractors' startled looks. "It's the same thing I've always done ever since building my first home in the early '60s with my cousin, Kenny Koll. I even did it in the custom home I built for my friend The Duke—that's John Wayne."

There was a moment of stunned silence.

"Well, I've got to get to the office. You guys work with Kathi." He looked toward me with a twinkle in his eyes. "And by the way, *yes*."

"What does *yes* mean?" one of the guys asked imitating his tone.

"She knows," Don replied, never taking his eyes off mine.

That bittersweet morning was the last time I saw Don as the man I knew on "the front side of the fence."

Don and I had planned an intimate dinner party for that evening at our home in Beverly Hills with our friends Susie Egans and the late, great Jerry Weintraub, the famous Hollywood producer. Jerry's list of interesting friends could fill a book, and we loved that our names were among those he held dearest. Don first met Jerry years earlier when they were amongst the first members to serve as President Reagan's presidential appointees to the Board of Trustees for The Kennedy Center in Washington, DC. They came from very different worlds, but bonded through mutual admiration for one another and a similar zest for life. We had recently run into Jerry, and he and Don talked about how fun it would be to rekindle their friendship. This was to be their reunion dinner and the path to a new friendship between Susie and me. Secretly, I had hoped we'd receive a last-minute call from Jerry pleading for us to include his pals George Clooney and Brad Pitt. Sadly, I was the one making the last-minute call.

I left Newport early to prepare our home in Beverly Hills for our little party. Traffic on the 405 between Newport Beach and Los Angeles was backing up, so I called Don to suggest leaving his office a little early to avoid the gridlock. Within minutes, he called me back and said, "I think you better call Jerry and cancel tonight." Don was the last one to ever cancel an engagement at the last minute, unless there was a darn good reason.

"Why?" I asked, more surprised than concerned at that point.

"I'm not feeling well," he said. "I'm feeling kind of punk." We had been in Scotland a few weeks earlier, and he hadn't felt well on the trip. He thought it was the flu and just couldn't seem to kick it.

"What are your symptoms?"

"Half of my face feels numb," he said. "My balance is off, and I've been slurring some words."

My heart sank, and my panic spiked. "Don, do you think you're having a stroke?" He said he didn't know but was about to leave for the hospital with his son-in-law.

A stroke had always been Don's biggest fear. Both his father and sister had died from them during their fifties, and Don battled the aching dread he would succumb to the same fate. He visited his doctor regularly, took prescribed medications, exercised with a trainer most mornings, and did everything he thought would help to avoid what he felt would one day be his demise. Sure enough, his actions and attention to health helped him live more than two decades longer than his father and sister. We often talked about the difference it made in our lives to lose family so young. We had to become stronger because they were no longer there for us to lean on.

He stayed on the phone with me while I raced off the freeway to turn around and head back south. He sounded OK, and as he spoke, I kept thinking this had to be a false alarm. He'd be fine. He was just being overly cautious. If there were a problem, surely everything would be OK because he was getting to the hospital within the crucial first three hours. He said he'd call me as soon as he registered, knowing it would be tough for me to get there beforehand with traffic. What normally could be a two-hour drive at rush hour took me only forty-five minutes. I'm a fast driver, but this time I broke all the rules—not only speeding, but also taking the carpool lane alone. Those forty-five minutes seemed like hours. I was so scared I wouldn't get to him in time for whatever was going to happen.

Finally, I drove into the hospital emergency entrance, parked, and ran through the swinging doors. I felt a rush of panic as I tried to find him. An administrator immediately took me into the ER where Don was lying on a gurney, just back from having a CAT Scan. We hugged each other tight. It was the first time I saw a look of fear in Don's eyes. That unsettling look from my Rock of Gibraltar scared me. Don the eternal optimist was scared, and he knew why. The doctor told him that there was a blood clot in his brain. The science-speak for what happened was a vertebral artery occlusion, which resulted in a medullary stroke. Basically, a blood clot in his brain caused him to have a brain stem stroke. A clot buster called T-PA was administered straight into the clot through his microcatheter. Over the coming years, I would speak the jargon just as fluently as the doctors.

Understandably nervous about having a stroke, Don and I had joined a group of friends at UCLA three months earlier for a private tour and lecture with the head of neurology. UCLA was the number-one stroke center in the country at the time, and Don was happy to know it was in our back yard. As we left the meeting he said, "If I ever have a stroke, I want you to know that, whatever it takes, I want to be here." Here we were at a different hospital, nowhere near where Don wanted to be. Hoag was our hospital of choice for many medical situations, but in 2005, their stroke center was small and brand new. It has grown immensely and is very impressive today, I might add. Don looked at me once again with that unsettling look in his eyes. I whispered in his ear, "You want to go to UCLA, don't you?"

"Yes," he said.

"Don't take this personally," I said as I told the doctor we wanted to helicopter Don out immediately. "It's because of our recent experience at UCLA and my husband's comfort level there. We don't know you, and you don't know us."

"You'll be losing precious time," the doctor said, reminding us of that critical three-hour window. "There's a good chance your husband won't make it that long. You will be taking a tremendous risk moving him."

"Don, this is your life. This decision has to be yours. I can't make it."

"Let's do it here," his voice was hardened with finality.

Before we could catch our breath, Don was being prepped for surgery. I didn't leave his side for a moment and felt as if I was about to go into surgery, too. It was me. It was him. It was us. We were one, and this was *our* problem. Whatever the outcome would be, no matter how frightened we were, we were in it together.

There was a lot of commotion. So many, many people coming and going. My mind was racing, my feelings raw, my everything swirling. The experience was so alien to me. I was trying to hang on. This couldn't be happening. I stayed close to Don and held his hand as he was wheeled down the hallway to surgery. But this was good that everything was happening so fast, right? He had done everything right. Time was on his side. Right? I just knew I'd see him again. This couldn't be the end.

Everything had been so perfect this morning. So incredibly beautiful.

He looked at me one last time before he was pushed through the heavy double doors to the operating room and said, "I love you."

I had no idea how long or how invasive the surgery would be. My family and Don's rushed to the hospital, where we all waited in one tiny waiting room as time was ticking, ticking, ticking away.

After the surgery, the doctor looked weary but determined. "Don's clot is as hard as a jawbreaker, but it's surrounded by a softer clot. Every effort has been made to extract it, but it is just too close to Don's brain stem, and the risk of removing all of it outweighs the chance of a piece breaking loose during surgery and damaging his brain stem. We could safely remove only the surrounding softer clot. Most of the clot has been removed, but there is still a part that will eventually have to be dealt with."

I had no idea what a brain stem was or what its function was. "I know my husband," I pleaded with him. "Go back in. No matter what it takes. He wouldn't want anything left; he'd go for broke." My inexperienced words fell upon deaf ears.

The next few hours felt like slow motion, a nightmare I couldn't wake up from. I didn't realize then that this was the beginning of my new life, a life that belonged in some obscure novel, not my reality. Not my life. Someone else's life. No, this couldn't possibly be me, be us.

My face was close to Don's as he opened his eyes. He was looking at me. He smiled. He knew me. The first thing he said was, "I love you."

Little by little, he regained consciousness, and during those late hours, I slowly started to believe all would be OK. The room was quiet, the lights dimmed. The doctor came in and explained the complication to Don. His utterly disappointed look of despair that the entire clot hadn't been removed was heartbreaking. I stayed with him quietly for a few hours, not knowing what to say. We both knew there was still something bad in his head. Once again, time was ticking, ticking, ticking.

Finally, Don broke the silence, "Kathi, you've got to go home and get some sleep."

"No way," I said. "I can't bear to leave you."

"Kathi, you need your sleep," he insisted. "We'll deal with this tomorrow. Look in my medicine cabinet. I have some Ambien. Take one and get a good night's sleep."

"Please, God, save him," I prayed as tears streamed down my face. "Please, God, don't take him from me. I need more time with him."

Just as Don had said, the Ambien sat on a shelf in his medicine cabinet. I stared at the bottle, realizing I had taken sleeping pills only for long airplane flights. Wonderful long flights meant an exciting place at the other end: Europe, Malaysia, Africa, South America. The list went on and on. Don had shown me the world. This time, I had no idea what world waited for me at the other end of sleep.

I looked around his small bathroom, touched the cool tile in front of his sink, and imagined him standing there only a few hours earlier. Who would ever imagine a man like Don Koll would be satisfied with a tiny old yellow-tiled bathroom with barely enough room to turn around in? It brought my thoughts back to the quietly charismatic man he really was. A man full of life without pretense. An ego big enough to bring illustrious success without making anyone feel like they were less. A true friend who always put family and so many others before himself and made everyone, be it a millionaire or a guy in the grocery store, feel like they were on his level. The man who let me be me. I grew up with self-confidence, but years of a not-so-perfect marriage with my first husband shattered that in many ways. When I met Don, I felt like a little bird in a cage. He opened that cage and let me fly.

I swallowed a pill using Don's water glass, which made me feel close to him. I quickly got ready for bed and, staring at Don's neatly made side, crawled under the sheets. I touched his pillow and cried myself to sleep, hoping the pill would take me out of my misery and into a few hours of emotionless rest.

I don't think I had been asleep for an hour when the piercing ring of the phone next to me pulled me out of the Ambien abyss. I'm not sure how long it rang; I had a hard time waking to answer it. There was a man's voice on the other end. "Is this Mrs. Koll?"

"Yes," I said in a fog.

"I'm so sorry to tell you this, but your husband has taken a turn for the worse. You need to get to the hospital as soon as possible."

"Is he alive?"

"Yes," he said. "But it's important you get here soon."

"Oh my God. No." I called my son, Kevin, right away.

"Mom, I'll meet you there. I'll be there, Mom."

I could hardly stand up from the effects of the sleeping pill. I couldn't think straight. I fell against the wall as I tried to pull on my jeans. I couldn't find my car keys and had no time to look for them. Sitting on the shelf behind our bed were the keys to Don's new little

Bentley. I grabbed them and ran down the stairs to the garage. It had been a huge decision for him to buy it, because he felt driving a Bentley looked too pretentious, but he loved the car. I said, "Come on, Don. If you want it, buy it. What do you care what people think?" I had never driven the car and didn't realize the power it had. The thought of what I did brings chills to me now, but I wasn't thinking about anything but getting to the hospital. Time was once again ticking, ticking, ticking.

I sped down the Pacific Coast Highway in the middle of the night and reached the hospital in record time. The back entrance was locked, and through sheer adrenaline, I pried it open and ran down the hall where Kevin was waiting for me. I fell into his arms sobbing. The doctor appeared within seconds.

"We have to go back in. We believe Don has had another stroke. We need to get the rest of the clot."

Kevin and I sat speechless in the waiting room, waiting to hear Don's fate. The doctor finally appeared in the doorway and asked me to follow him into a small room where the X-ray of Don's brain was hanging in front of a light. He was encouraged that there was no clot.

Yes, it was gone, but we soon discovered that as it exited his brain through his blood stream, it damaged his brain stem.

We were now on the back side of the fence, the back side of the mountain, but it wasn't the bottom of the sea.

I distinctly remember Don saying to me one day, "You know, Kathi, there are only three things in life that really matter: food, water, and love. Food and water enable one to exist. Love enables one to live." I would imagine his buddies would be surprised by the simplicity of these words, but then again, maybe not. His close friends understood the depth of his feelings; only the outer fringe would have been surprised.

Those words resonated with me more than he knew at the time, and the strength of them was tucked away deep in my thoughts, to reappear after Don was ill.

Before Don, I never knew anyone who had suffered a stroke. In some ways, maybe that was a good thing, because I innocently felt if I did all I could and helped Don keep up his enthusiasm, we'd be back to our normal life within six months. I never knew anyone disabled, either. I had an unfair amount of experience with death and dying in my family, but I had no idea what someone disabled and possibly doomed to a quadriplegic life would possibly be like. Those thoughts didn't even enter my mind then, because I thought Don would be "fixed" within six months, and this nightmare would be behind us.

I couldn't bear to leave Don alone at the hospital in those first few weeks, but the lack of sleep was taking a toll on me. One of Don's doctors, Dr. Michael Brant-Zawadzki, took me aside and said, "Kathi, you need some rest. Life is now going to be a marathon, not a sprint."

I had no idea what he was talking about. The days and nights rolled into one.

The fear in Don's eyes when he first opened them is still burned into my memory. He didn't need to move or show expression; everything came through his eyes. They were piercing, frightened, helpless, and hopeless. I could feel him, sense him, and hear him. Not through voice or touch—only by the look in his eyes.

It's hard to explain the true pain of it all or how either of us survived, but there was constant hope that threatened to be toppled by many disappointments. I counted the days and the minutes for any kind of movement to return. The first eighteen hours, I did not take my eyes off his toes. "You can do it, Don. Think of your days at Stanford when you were on the swim team, kicking your legs as hard as you could while gliding across the pool. Think of pulling back on the throttle of the

F-86F fighter jet you flew in the Air Force. Think hard. Imagine you're in your Porsche pushing down on the pedal to change gears. Think. Imagine. You can do it. Think. Imagine." He tried so hard. Once again, I could see the determination in his eyes. The bewitching time was upon us and nothing.

The same problems affecting his movement were also affecting his breathing. He was put onto a ventilator with the hopes his diaphragm would regain its function within days. "Don, you can breathe. Think. Imagine. You can do it. Remember when you'd hold your breath while skiing? When you reached the bottom of the run, you gasped for breath, filling your lungs with air as if it was your first. Remember? You can do it again. It's a memory, you know. Do it again. Please. You can do it."

It was exhausting waiting for Don to move a toe, a finger, give an expression on his face, breathe. Every little goal reached was like climbing Mt. Everest, only the summit was always so very far away, and time was ticking, ticking, ticking away. Every day that passed was a slow realization that life would never be the same.

My heart was full of love and so full of pain. I couldn't stop crying every time I left his room, but I couldn't let him see me that way. I had to be brave for him; I had to give him hope, and the only way to do that was for him to derive strength from my positive attitude. Surely he would think he was going to get better if he saw the positive and unwavering optimism I had for him.

I was so scared, sad, confused, and helpless, but I was determined to keep it all secret. He couldn't know any of it. I sat close to him, holding his hand, passing my hand gently over his forehead. I kissed his cheeks, his lips, and gently rested my face against his. All the while, my heart filled with sadness, which I knew his was feeling, too. I could see it in his eyes. I could see it when I wiped away his tears. My Rock of Gibraltar was silently crying, and it broke my heart. How could I make him happy? How could I give him strength? I started to realize that this would be my job. I would be in charge, but never let him know he wasn't. Till the day he died, he was to be in charge and take care of me, which he did so many times with only the strength of his eyes.

My friend Alexandre de Borchgrave had recently written a book of poetry about love and life in honor of 9/11. I spotted it on the bookshelf one morning and grabbed it as I was scurrying off to the hospital, thinking it might be soothing for Don to listen to me read it to him. I quickly learned how much my reading meant to him. When the lights dimmed late at night in the ICU, I read it to him, and right before I left, I whispered a special memory we shared into his ear. Quietly I'd ask him to think of that memory as he went to sleep, and I would do the same. In a life that lost all privacy, these were our own special secrets never to be shared. Every night another memory took us away from our bleak reality and back into a world of happiness.

5

LOCKED IN

"My diving bell becomes less oppressive, and my mind takes flight like a butterfly."
—Jean-Dominique Bauby

There's no better description of our life than the one depicted in the French book-turned-movie *The Diving Bell and the Butterfly*. When Don first had his stroke, a friend recommended I read the book. The story is about Jean-Dominique Bauby, editor of the French fashion magazine *ELLE*, who suffered the same type of stroke as Don with the same devastating results, albeit Jean-Dominique never left the hospital. I'm glad I didn't read it in the beginning. I wasn't ready to witness the reality I was living.

I finally relented in 2007, two years after Don's stroke, when the movie came out. I had experimented with all sorts of ways to help Don communicate and thought if I saw the film I'd learn something. I really didn't know much about the story. If I had known, I might not have gone. My two girls, Jennifer and Brooke, insisted on going with me, knowing I would need tremendous support. The three of us sat together stunned, holding hands and trying to hold back our tears as we watched the story unfolding onscreen. It was my life; it was our family's life, and it was Don's life. The similarities were uncanny. I went home with the gift of seeing the story through the patient's eyes.

As sad and difficult as it was for me to watch, I took away a very, very important lesson. Jean-Dominique couldn't move, but he was the same man inside. It was the first time I really focused on the fact that the world looked the same from Don's vantage point. He was looking out as he always had; only now, he looked different to all of *us*. Don couldn't move, but he was the same man he had always been with the same intelligence and unwavering optimism for life.

The movie gave me an entirely new way to look at people with disabilities. In the film, Jean's old friends visited but looked at and treated him as if he was a child or had amnesia. They put their faces close to him and said, "Jean-Dominique, I'm your old friend, Pierre. We went to school together." Jean peered at this friend, saying to himself, *What's wrong with you, you old fool? Of course I know who you are.*

Like Jean-Dominique, Don started his day as he started any other day, and in a matter of seconds, it changed forever. Don awakened from his surgery completely "locked in." He couldn't speak, couldn't move, couldn't breathe. The touchstone of my life couldn't do anything other than look at me, and the look in his eyes was one of total fear. For the first time he was looking towards me as his rock. His mind was intact, but that was all, and at that moment, I wondered if that was a good thing or not.

I'm not sure when he first realized his plight or the innermost thoughts going through his mind. I did recently learn that Don used to mouth to the nurses, "You know, this is my bonus life." He never mouthed that to me. When I heard that, so many raw emotions opened up. I found comfort in knowing from those words that he knew he was supposed to die and was living a life he never expected to have, a bonus few get to enjoy. I find comfort looking back on how much he embraced the opportunity. If he hadn't, he would have closed his eyes many years earlier. Don made it very clear over and over again that he wanted to live.

Time and time again people asked the hurtful question, "Why didn't you just pull the plug?" One woman even said to me, "I'd never let my husband live like that." I probably would have reacted that way, too, if I had not lived through it and come to understand the difference between being brain dead and being the same person without the ability to move. The hurtful conclusion people were alluding to is called murder. It's the attitude that begs the question, "Why don't you make your life and his life easier?" Life, unfortunately, can't always just be a convenience.

When Don awakened, I stroked his forehead with my hand, leaned over, and kissed his cheek. I kissed his lips as I always did. He kissed me back. I could feel his pain, his fear.

It was a story I only saw in the movies. Not a story of normal people like us.

In the cubicle next to Don at UCLA was a beautiful young Swiss girl who was in a coma. My thoughts turned to her often, especially in those first months of recovery as life seemed so unreal. The actor Robert Wagner and his wife, actress Jill St. John, visited her regularly because she was taking care of their horses at the time of her accident. She left their barn with one of the horses, and it came back without her. She was found unconscious on the side of the road in a canyon I grew up in riding horses as a child. We knew RJ and Jill casually, and they stopped by to see me and give encouragement to us as they passed by our little section on their way to see this young girl. They were incredible with her and took care of her as if she were their child. Her parents arrived from Switzerland not speaking much English. I sat in the waiting room with them hours upon hours. My heart bled for this mother and father in a strange country with a beautiful young girl barely alive and in a deep coma.

"Would you like to meet her?" they asked in their best English.

"Yes, I am honored that you are asking me." I took them to Don's bedside first and shared our story in my broken French and the little bit of English they could understand. "This is my husband, Don." I had told him all about their beautiful daughter, so he understood who they were and their unquestionable compassion and hope. He used every bit of energy to give them a slight smile. It was all he could do to show his respect.

They guided me into their daughter's small room. The walls were covered with family photos and pictures of her favorite horses, music they knew she liked playing quietly in the background. They gestured to step closer so they could introduce her to me. She loved the small canyon where her accident happened, and since I'd grown up there, her parents felt it would make her feel closer to me.

"I grew up in a very special little spot in Los Angeles called Sullivan Canyon, where I rode horses and she had her accident. As a child, I thought I was the oddball of my friends. They had sidewalks in front of their homes, and I lived in a canyon with a stream, hiking trails, and horses. Of course it was just the opposite—my friends envied me for living in 'the country.'" I squeezed her hand and whispered into her ear. "I used to ride up the trails beyond the hiking paths of Sullivan Canyon, over the mountain and deep into Rustic Canyon with my friend Cecily Waycott. We would put our cans of soft drinks into the stream to stay cold as we rode on up the canyon before riding back to sit by the bank to eat our lunch. I'll cherish those idle days of summer, riding my horse everyday." If she could hear me, maybe she could relate to this, and maybe the magical descriptions might take her into a cloud of happiness. I tried to think of anything I could do to make the afternoon somewhat normal, which was anything but. She was an incredibly beautiful young girl who had been robbed of her life.

6

OUR NEW NORMAL

*"Normality is a paved road: It's comfortable to walk,
but no flowers grow on it."*
—Vincent van Gogh

When am I going to wake up?" I was crying, sweating, screaming. I couldn't breathe. "I want to wake up. I want out of this nightmare. I'm sick of people saying, 'You're so strong. I could never be so strong.' I don't want to be strong. I don't want this to happen to me. What do you think I'm going to do, people? What choice do I have?"

I felt like I was in a nightmare, but I couldn't escape because I was awake in my new reality. I had no idea what that meant or what lay ahead for me, but I was awake and couldn't go back to the life I knew.

A nurse came in and gently whispered into my ear that a priest was outside. *My God, a priest is here for Don's last rites*, I thought.

"Is he dying?" I asked. The doctor had said he wouldn't live through the night, and when he did, the doctor said he wouldn't live long, but I was optimistic. "It must be the end," I said to the nurse.

She squeezed my hand and said, "Monsignor Baird would like to visit Don."

Monsignor Baird walked in, wrapped his arms around me, then gently put his hand on Don's shoulder. His words were words of comfort, not the last rites. Comforting thoughts before praying by Don's bedside. Don's eyes never left the priest, and I could see in them a feeling of comfort, of safety. Don wasn't an overly religious person, but that night, I saw him embrace pure spirituality for the first time.

At first, Don and I could only communicate through the blinking of his eyes. "Don, give me one blink for yes and two blinks for no. Don, let's look at this like a sporting event. We're on the same team, and I mean to win. Give me one blink if you're in or two blinks if you don't want to play the game." I've never been keen on calling an illness a war, and I felt better thinking we were going into a competition. He closed his eyes tightly and then opened them once with determination. I knew he was in and wanted to live. For the rest of his life, the doctors would question him regularly and ask if he wanted to be resuscitated in case of an emergency. He always indicated yes. Don wanted to live, and live he did.

As days turned into nights and nights turned into days, I started to realize that things weren't going to change as rapidly as I had thought. Don's doctor took me aside and said, "Kathi, you need to take care of yourself, or you're going to burn out." I needed sleep, but the thought of leaving Don alone in a hospital full of strangers was frightening. I came up with the idea of having family and friends spend each night with Don so he wouldn't be alone. The answer to my request was overwhelming. Family and friends from junior high school, college, and business signed up and rotated sleeping next to Don on a small cot night after night in the ICU. The comfort it brought to both of us—especially Don—was indescribable. Even Don's college friend Ron Tomsic took shifts, despite having just endured a double knee replacement. He brought bags of ice to put on his knees while lying on the cot next to Don. It gave him a sense of security and kept him from feeling alone. Throughout the years, he had given so selflessly to others, it was inspiring to see him receive that support from others now. It was a show of love towards him he never knew existed.

As days and then weeks marched on, Don's face regained movement. From the neck up he was starting to look like his handsome self again and could mouth words. He talked like he always did, but without a voice; it became a frustration that haunted us the rest of his life. I soon learned that many words are formed the same way, but the sounds are different. He'd get so incredibly frustrated if I couldn't read his lips. There were many attempts to use cutting-edge tech like eye-gaze technology, and even doctors from other hospitals who truly believed they could help Don speak again gave their best efforts; but it just wasn't in the cards for us. We tried as many suggestions as seemed reasonable for Don's condition, but in the end, we had our own language and communication that we made work for us. I devised a spelling board to use when it was impossible to understand him solely through lip reading. He hated it, but boy oh boy, when he wanted himself understood, he'd use the board for as long as it took. The board was numbered down the left side, and each number had a line with letters of the alphabet:

1 A B C D
2 E F G H
3 I J K L
4 M N O P
5 Q R S T
6 U V W
7 X Y Z

I asked him to mouth which line the first letter of the word was on. Once we got the line, I pointed to letters one at a time, and he'd mouth the one he needed. When I choose the correct letter, I wrote it on a white board for him to see, and we would move on to the next letter. A sentence could sometimes take thirty minutes. One day, Tom Foster, his friend and attorney of many years, was at our home. Don was intent on Tom understanding every thought he was conveying. Tom left dripping in sweat and said, "Kathi, how do you do it?" It was nice to know someone else understood the frustration and stamina it took. Not only was Don determined to live, he was in charge of his life and his ideas. His thoughts were his and his alone. I was attracted to his strength from the outset, but now his strength was more impressive than ever.

Way before Don's stroke, I was sitting next to our friend Mike Niven at a dinner party. He said to me, "You know, Kathi, Don is one of the few guys I can describe as a man, not a boy, and there are very few of them." He was so right. He was my John Wayne, my knight in shining armor, the man on the white horse.

Days turned into weeks. There were slight improvements, but few, and time wasn't on our side. Each day that Don didn't regain movement was closer to the reality that he never would.

Our story quickly made news in our community. All sorts of stories were flying around, and word spread quickly from coast to coast. At first, no one knew what kind of fight Don was really up against both physically and emotionally, but support came rolling in as soon as everyone knew. I even received a lovely orchid and letter from Prince Charles. Among the hundreds of emails and letters I received were two separate, very heartfelt ones from President and Mrs. Bush. They couldn't believe how great Don had looked and acted so recently, and now his life was hanging by a thread. Of all the letters from the people we felt so fortunate to have connected with, one that has always stood out to me was from a total stranger. A man wrote to us saying that Don had helped him change his tire on the side of the road one night. He said that he never expected a man like Don to stop for a man like him, but that was the striking thing about Don: He made everyone feel important because he treated every person like they were special. It was so touching to see the breadth of people he affected with his kindness and generosity.

Catherine Ross, a local doctor, heard what happened and invited me to come to her home to meet her and her husband. He had suffered an injury when he was thrown off his horse and had become a quadriplegic, although he was not on a respirator. That was the day reality hit me like a ton of bricks. My entire family—Jennifer, Kevin, Brooke, and brother Don—accompanied me to their home about forty-five minutes from ours.

"Oh my God, there's a ramp." The pit that had been growing in my stomach during the drive to the Ross home solidified and sank. Jennifer, Kevin, Brooke, and my brother Don and I walked up to the door and rang the bell. A man in a wheelchair answered. I had never met anyone like him before. His wife, Catherine, stood beside him, and together they welcomed us into their home. He wasn't on a respirator, so he could talk, a luxury Don never regained. He operated his wheelchair by blowing through a straw. Graciously, he gave us a tour of their home and explained how he lived day in and day out.

He started by showing us the Hoyer lift that lifted him from his chair to his bed, then took us to see how his van was outfitted with a hydraulic lift to place him and his wheelchair next to the driver. I was overwhelmed with gratitude that complete strangers reached out to help, but at the same time, I did everything I could to not cry as he showed us how he turned on his TV and lights. This couldn't be happening to me. To us. *Please, God, help me,* I silently screamed. I didn't see how I could do this, and I didn't want to.

I returned to the hospital shaken from the experience and nervous to talk to Don. He knew where I was going, but I felt certain he wasn't ready to hear the grim details. I feared he'd lose hope. The minute I arrived, he was intent on telling me something. It was obvious he was anxious and determined for me to understand him. I held up the spelling board, and he blinked one letter at a time until I could read his message: *You have to get me to UCLA, or I will die.*

UCLA was—and probably still is—the number-one stroke center in the country, and I knew Don felt his best chance for any kind of recovery was to be in a major hospital. Arranging for Don to be transferred to the ICU Neurology Unit of the UCLA Ronald Reagan Medical Center within a few days was no small feat. Because the unit was small, we had to wait for a spot to become available, and there was a lot of red tape on both ends. Finally, after almost missing our opportunity when the bed originally intended for Don was filled, we made the slow drive from Newport Beach to UCLA by ambulance when another bed opened up within a few days. Dr. Yince Loh, the Fellow studying under the head of the unit, Dr. Paul Vespa, admitted Don. Over the next three months, I camped out at the hospital. Everyone knew me, and I knew all of the staff. It became my life, and I very quickly grew to understand and respect the incredible dedication of the medical world.

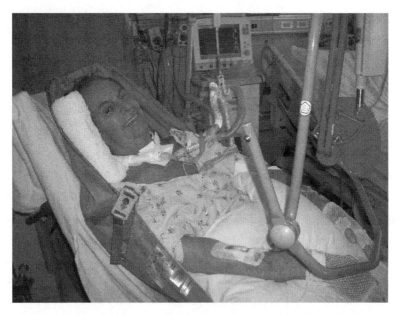

Smiling through his challenge—forever the optimist

Early one Sunday morning after having been in the ICU for a few weeks, one of Don's main doctors, Dr. Robert Shpiner, called me and asked if I could meet him in the cafeteria. My heart sank. *Please no*, I thought. *Please no more bad news.*

I could have asked any number of willing family members or friends to accompany me, but for some reason I felt that I needed to go alone and face whatever he was about to say to me. My gut said it wasn't good. Dr. Shpiner was sitting at a table towards the back of the room. I took a seat across from him, and he uttered those dreaded words. "Does your husband have all his affairs in order?"

I was shocked at what I was hearing. This was UCLA. This was the place my husband felt confident in. They were going to fix him, save him. Why was Dr. Shpiner saying these dreaded words to me? Following my life-changing discussion with Dr. Shpiner believing Don wouldn't last long, days rolled into weeks and then into months. Don defied the doctors yet again. He was gathering believers.

I never thought about our next step. I wasn't counting the days, weeks, or months that we had been at UCLA. Time didn't seem to exist. One afternoon, Dr. Vespa took me aside and said, "It's time for Don to move. He's stable, and we can't do any more for him. We're not a convalescent hospital." I had no idea what to do. He scribbled a few suggestions on a piece of paper and handed it to me.

I was stunned. He wasn't fixed. Where were we going to go? I called our good friend Dr. Ken Horacek who had been a sounding board to me from the start. He had a few suggestions, but few places take patients on a respirator. Our close friend Jim "Watty" Watson, who had been a source of strength to me and Don, visited one place for me, but afterward he called and said, "No way in hell can DK go there." I was at my wit's end. Don had no idea the dilemma we were facing, and I didn't think it was wise to share it with him.

Two of my best girlfriends, Nettie Dart and Chery Horacek, Dr. Horacek's wife, volunteered to visit some prospective places with me. There were only two that were willing to accept Don. The three of us climbed into Nettie's car and took off. The first place was hesitant when they heard Don's condition. The second was a little more willing and tried to console me by telling me that every afternoon Don would be wheeled into an arts and crafts session that they were sure he'd love. *Arts and crafts,* I thought, *they have to be kidding.* My husband, who a mere three months ago was traveling the world and running a successful business, was going to spend the rest of his life watching someone making teepees with Popsicle sticks?

The three of us walked to the parking structure. My girlfriends had their arms around me. I knew they were holding back tears, but I was outright sobbing.

Time was running away from me, and I couldn't catch it. The hospital was putting pressure on me, and I had absolutely no idea what I was going to do. I was ducking the doctors for fear the subject would come up. I finally sat down next to Don and tenderly shared our dilemma. He looked at me and mouthed, "I want to go home."

Home? It hadn't crossed my mind. How in the world could I ever make that happen?

7

THERE'S NO PLACE
LIKE HOME

*"What counts is not necessarily the size of the dog in the fight—
it's the size of the fight in the dog."*
—Dwight Eisenhower

I would like to move Don home. How could we possibly make that happen?" If Don wanted to be home, I at least wanted to see if it was an option.

"I'll bring it up with the team, but to be frank, I can't imagine it working," Don's doctor told me. I wasn't sure who "the team" was "Basically, in order for us to release Don home instead of to a facility, our decision will have to be unanimous."

I must have looked frustrated because his face softened.

"We'll call a meeting to discuss it with you."

Dr. Vespa found the idea unlikely and felt he'd be back in the hospital within a week. Dr. Dobkin, who was in charge of Don's rehab, was a positive, but Don's main doctor, Dr. Shpiner, also had his doubts. The lack of enthusiasm made me nervous for the meeting, but I was determined to sway them. I walked into a conference room at the appointed time and found about twenty people sitting on either side of what seemed like a very long table. The sight of all these people really shook me up. I wasn't ready to discuss Don's situation with so many strangers. I thought I was just meeting with the three doctors, so I felt completely blindsided. As their questions started coming at me like darts—albeit tactful darts—I started to cry. Someone slid a box of tissue in front of me, but I couldn't stop crying. The additional people were actually there to discuss all sorts of care for Don and had great intentions, but I just wasn't emotionally prepared for that conversation. It was evident that we wouldn't be able to get done what we needed to, so the meeting was canceled and rescheduled for the next day.

I called my friend Dr. Horacek, and he recommended that his wife, Chery, and my close friend Nettie Dart go to the meeting the next day with me for support, especially since they had helped me evaluate alternative facilities. I'm not sure I could have done it without them. I was taking a huge step trying to bring Don home, and their emotional help during the meeting was tremendous. I needed "a team" too. The same group was at the long table, but this time I felt stronger and ready for them. *Sort of.*

After much negative discussion, I finally said, "This is UCLA, and you're supposed to be a teaching hospital, right? Instead of fighting me on this, why can't everyone come together and help me? Maybe this teaching hospital will learn something from our experience."

Dr. Shpiner was starting to come around.

"What are you going to do if the electricity goes out at your house?" Dr. Vespa asked. "Don will only live a short time without his respirator working."

"I've already thought of that and have bought a backup generator," I replied coolly and confidently.

"Does Don realize he probably won't live long doing this?" he asked. "There are just too many obstacles and possible emergency situations."

"Why don't we all just walk down the hall. We can ask Don what he thinks."

Drs. Dobkin, Shpiner, and Vespa followed me into Don's small cubicle in the ICU. Don listened to all the pros and cons (mostly cons) coming from the doctors.

"Don," Dr. Vespa finally really looked at him, "there's a good chance you'll die at home if you do this."

Without a second of a hesitation Don mouthed, "I want to go home. I understand. I would rather die at home."

With that, all three doctors went into action and said they'd help me make it happen. It was forward momentum, and for us, that was a breath of fresh air.

For months, I had been watching all the medical personnel working with Don very closely. Nurses, respiratory therapists, physical and occupational therapists, speech therapists, care helpers. I knew who I liked, who was good, and most importantly, who Don liked and didn't like. A number of the nurses and respiratory therapists had jobs outside of UCLA on their days off, so I started approaching the ones I felt would be a good fit with the idea of working at our home on their off days. "Come on, just try it," I would say. "I promise it won't be a miserable job, and I won't be difficult to work for. We have a pool you can relax by on your time off." Was that ever a naive statement! But it sounded good at the time—I was selling and selling hard.

I found a wonderful doctor, Dr. Harley Liker, to come on board the first year and help me coordinate with Dr. Shpiner on Don's care. I was able to put a small team together, and from there it grew. I had no idea how to order medical supplies, equipment, clothes, or any of the other myriad of things I discovered we needed, but together we started making it work. We were the DK Team, and once people signed up, they were committed. Scheduling was overwhelming. Don could never be left alone, so there couldn't be any gaps on the calendar. With time, my makeshift medical center ran like clock-work, but oh how complicated it was medically and emotionally in the beginning.

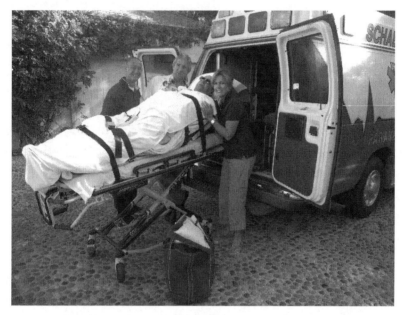

Finally home

The day, then the hour descended upon us, and there was so much more to do. I was anxious to make it work and couldn't wait to get Don home; but at the same time, it scared me to death. Lists were being checked, crossed out, and double-checked. Just getting the right hospital bed was a challenge. Who would have thought I needed a bed with a scale? Well, of course I did. Don couldn't stand on a scale, and taking his weight every day was important. Just getting the huge Stryker bed into the house was a challenge. It took twelve men. The supplies were mind-boggling. The custom wheelchair to fit Don's unique situation as a quadriplegic, the lift to get him into the chair and/or bed, the standing board, whatever in the world that was, the chucks under him to roll him from side to side when dressing him, the leg compressions, thermometers, syringes, a defibrillator, extra tracheotomy tubes (or trachs) for emergencies, poles to hang IVs... The list went on and on and on.

Don's situation meant 24/7 care, and he could never be alone for the rest of his life. This kind of care wasn't going to be paid for by insurance and didn't come cheap. Fortunately, Don's success prior to his stroke made all of the necessary care financially feasible. Right from the outset I told him, "Don, I just want you to know that if we need to spend every last penny you've made, it's OK with me. You made it, and this is the time in your life that you should spend it to give yourself the best life possible." I could see relief in his smile as he mouthed, "I love you."

I stood next to him in the ICU as we waited for all the paperwork to be completed. Don's patience wore thinner the longer it took. Finally, we were off. Before this, I didn't know that one could "hire" an ambulance, but over the next several years, we did it hundreds of times. I wondered what Don was thinking as he looked out the back windows of the ambulance at so many familiar sights. Trees, homes, and buildings he most likely always took for granted. Now he was seeing them with another chance at life, and the dream of going home becoming a reality. As we drove into our driveway for the first time after so many long and emotional months, I couldn't help but feel a bit proud that I was making it happen. So many months, so many serious health scares, so many people saying, "He'll never go home again," and "He won't live long," and here we were.

Dr. Shpiner was there to make sure all went smoothly, as he did for the rest of Don's life, along with Dr. Liker. About an hour later, Dr. Dobkin arrived. He sat in the living room with me for quite a while trying to calm any fear I had. "Kathi," he said earnestly, "make sure Don doesn't just live to exist. Make sure he exists to live." It became my theme for the kind of life I would help Don have for the rest of his life. This was our new normal, and I was determined to make both our lives as normal as possible.

Part of looking normal was making sure our room didn't look like a hospital, so I insisted that all supplies needed close to Don be put into our beautiful antique side tables. Someone recommended that I roll up our area rug and work on the hardwood floor so that spills would be easy to mop up. "No," I insisted. "Everyone needs to be a little more careful. We can always have the carpet cleaned, but our room and life are going to be as normal as possible."

Hospital Central was in the guest bedroom next to our room. We stored some often-needed supplies there, and the medical crew made it their headquarters. The bulk of the supplies took over our garage. On top of our home overflowing with medical supplies, the laundry never stopped, which was only made worse because I had so little time to do it. There was so much I had to buy an additional washer and dryer.

I still believed Don would be back to normal in six months and off the respirator in a week or so. I rearranged our third bedroom as my own temporary living space, never thinking I would stay with Don in our home ICU, but when I mentioned it, the disappointment on his face was too much for me to take. There went my little space of privacy, but I loved the fact he never had a second thought about me being right there with him. I couldn't bear being far from him anyway. It was just another part of our new normal.

I moved our king-sized bed into storage, but I kept the beautiful fabric-covered headboard behind Don's hospital bed. I had to improvise and used the blow-up mattress we had for the grandkids. I ended up sleeping on it for nine months—I optimistically thought everything would get back to the way it was, so why buy another bed? Every night, Don practically barked at the nurses to help get my bed blown up. He was always trying, in the only way he could, to take care of me.

Going to sleep that first night Don came home was a bit awkward. I always slept in a nightgown, but I was in a room with complete strangers, one of whom was a man. I couldn't wear a nightgown in front of these people. In all the careful preparations made to bring Don home, I had overlooked that logistic. Surely I had some forgotten set of pajamas in my bottom drawer. Negative. I found my old grey sweatshirt and sweatpants instead. I also came across some of the provocative little teddies I'd wear with him. In the midst of the overcrowded hubbub that had become our bedroom, I gave myself a private moment to cry as I wondered if I would ever wear them with him again.

Putting sheets on the blow-up bed was like living a scene from a Chaplin film, but I didn't think it was funny. I'd wrangle them around one corner, and they would slide off as soon as I moved on to the next. I couldn't let that get in the way of the elation I felt being back in my own bedroom with the man I loved, so I went into the garage and got my sleeping bag. I could hardly believe that after months without Don in our bedroom, I was finally sleeping with him again—albeit on a blow-up mattress, in a sleeping bag, wearing sweats, with strangers watching me. It was all so weird and unreal, but I was in dreamland having Don home, right next to me with my arm around him.

Just one short month later, we all got an amazing little dose of joy—something Jennifer has always seemed to bring in the most difficult times. I remember the birth of each of my grandchildren just as vividly as the births of each of my own children. In my day, not many of us knew ahead of time what sex the baby was going to be, but nowadays, it's only a mystery if you enjoy the surprise like my daughter Jennifer. Her first baby—and my first grandchild—was a boy named

Flynn, and eighteen months later he was joined by "Little Kathi." Her birth came only a few months after Don's debilitating stroke. The entire family was looking forward to her arrival with more excitement than usual. A day to escape the misery at home and welcome a new life into our family.

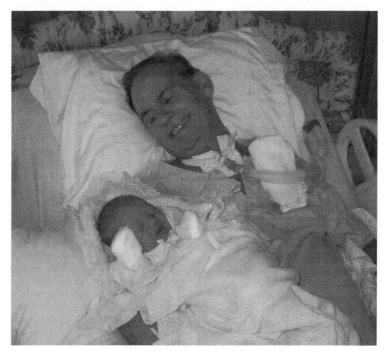

Don and baby Kathi

Before Don's stroke, Jennifer had stopped by the house holding an envelope.

"Mom, the doctor just gave me the report showing the sex of my baby. It's in this envelope. I just don't think I can have it at my home without peeking inside. Would you take it and store it away for me?" She bolted out of the house just as quickly as she'd popped the question. I stood in the kitchen staring at the envelope mustering up all my strength to not look inside.

What made her think I could resist? I thought. While I was staring at it, I heard Don coming in the front gate from work. "What are you looking at, Kathi?"

"Well, this envelope contains the sex of Jennifer and Rick's baby."

With lightning speed he grabbed the envelope out of my hands. "I think I'd better take this and hide it away before you cave and look inside."

That was that. The secret would be safe with him.

Exactly four months after the stroke, the baby was due to arrive. I was so excited to greet my new little grandbaby into this world that I awoke early. Don was already awake and staring at me. The minute I caught his eye he gave me a big smile. He knew the day of the C-section had finally arrived, and the thought of a precious little baby would bring joy to all of us.

I dressed quickly and raced to the hospital. The entire family arrived full of anticipation and excitement. We all had our guesses of what the baby would be. I took my place in the delivery room alongside my son-in-law, Rick, as I had done for Flynn's birth. Within minutes I heard the doctor announce, "You have a beautiful little baby girl." Rick headed out to the waiting room to tell everyone, with me in tow.

I arrived home in the early afternoon, anxious to share the news with Don. "So," I asked, "what do you think the baby is?"

"I know what it is," he mouthed with a sly little smile.

"Well then, what it is?"

"A girl," he quickly answered.

"How do you know?"

"I peeked. I've known all along."

My jaw hit the ground. He was the guardian of the secret and had opened the envelope within minutes of taking it from me. I was glad he did. I think it gave him a lot of pleasure knowing we didn't know that he knew as he listened to us speculate month after month.

I couldn't help but think, *Good for Don. Here he is paralyzed and on a respirator, but he still has a great sense of humor.*

Of all Don's legacies, the one that touches my heart the most is how he influenced the grandchildren. They spent their formative years with "Grandpa in the Wheelchair," which has given them a level of comfort and familiarity around disability that many children their age will never experience. They'll grow up with the opportunity to share that empathy with others.

8

THE TEST

"You may have to fight a battle more than once to win it."
—Margaret Thatcher

In some ways, the first eighteen months were the most difficult. The adjustment period of our new life was the most challenging I've ever experienced. My home was a small world within itself. It didn't take me long to respect the staff who cared for Don. They loved him and it showed. The saddest challenge was Don's fear I'd leave him, and boy did he put me to the test. I learned later that testing people was innate to him. I even witnessed it firsthand shortly after he had his stroke, when a business associate unsuccessfully tried to take over his company.

Sometimes it takes something catastrophic to make a change in one's life. Yes, my life changed when Don had his stroke, but that was his test. Mine came a bit later and practically put me over the edge. I had felt depression before, like a wounded bird looking up at a wobbly branch after a gust of wind. How could I not have, with everything that I had already been through?

I felt that unbearable pain and fragility at Don's bedside. I had survived so many hardships, but this new kind of pain was uncontrollable.

Within the first four or five months of Don's stroke, he asked me out of the blue if I'd like to have a boyfriend. I was shocked and hurt by the question, which put his feelings to rest. "Are you kidding, Don?" I sobbed. "How could you possibly ask me that? What would put that question in your mind?"

I wondered if he was being unselfish or testing my loyalty. I must admit that during the first eighteen months after his illness, I was missing a physical life more than I ever thought possible. I didn't share these feelings with Don, other than to tell him that the smell of him still sent me into orbit. It was true, and I thought sharing this with him would make him feel good about himself. It did make him smile. The loss of intimacy was driving me crazy, but time brought on a numbness that was a welcomed respite. I guess the expression "If you don't use it, you lose it" came true, but in my case, it was a God-given present. The thought of being unfaithful to Don didn't enter my thoughts for a moment, but fantasies of him were what helped me carry on as I closed my eyes for the few precious hours of sleep between awakening to help turn him or an alarm going off from one of his machines.

After 9 months of sleeping on a blow-up mattress I graduated to a hospital bed. Weird as it seems to picture two hospital beds pushed together, we had some wonderful evenings. Someone told me that laughter was an important ingredient to wellness, so I purchased a DVD of Robin Williams. Don was loving every minute of the show. I could hear his silent laughter. Once the show was over, I helped ready him for bed. I crawled under my sheets with my bed pushed next to his and stretched my arm across his chest, burying my hand behind his neck—a habit no hospital bed could break. I cuddled up to him as much as possible, knowing if the beds moved slightly I'd fall between the crack; but as I closed my eyes, I could feel only the closeness of his body, his illness a million miles away. We had spent the evening laughing, and now we were in our own little unconventional dream world.

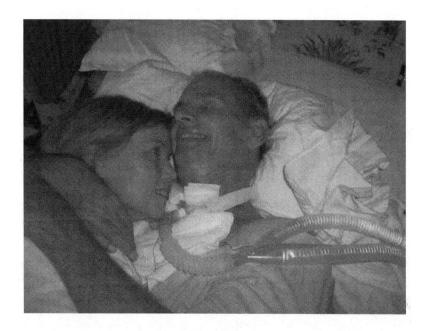

I awakened early as usual and forced myself to quickly get out of bed. If I stayed too long in my little cocoon, I'd start thinking about too many things that would turn my few blissful hours of sleep to sadness. Even now, if I lie in bed too long, my thoughts get the better of me, and the shadow of a sad cloud can freeze me from moving forward. The day started like all the rest but quickly turned very dark. Don was angry with me. This had happened before, and I realized that even though he had been happy when he went to sleep, he had 24/7 to think, think, think, and that could take him a million miles away. He thought about every second of his life, and he now had the time to do so.

This particular morning, he was unusually agitated with me. I couldn't imagine why. We'd had a fun evening the night before. He was happy; I was happy. We had only gone to sleep, albeit awakened for medical reasons a few times within the early-morning hours. Now he was looking at me with deep disdain.

"Don, are you upset?" I asked.

"Yes," he mouthed.

"Are you upset with me? Did I do something wrong?"

"Yes."

"I only went to sleep. I helped you through the night. What could I have possibly done to upset you?"

"I saw you," he mouthed. "I saw you get in that black car with that guy in our front courtyard. I saw that same guy at the restaurant at another table waiting for you."

"Why are you saying this to me, Don?" This was a nightmare I never imagined. He was breaking my heart. It was all untrue, but he was adamant and impossible to reason with. The hurt I was feeling was so far beyond anything I could ever explain. I had done nothing. If I had, I would have felt better—I would have been failing at some kind of a cover-up for unfaithfulness; but the reality was that these accusations had come out of nowhere.

He wouldn't let up. I was sobbing so hard I could feel myself gasping for breath. He showed no sympathy for my tears. I was giving my every living moment to this man, the love of my life, who had just turned on me, and why?

"Why, Don?" I questioned. "Where is this coming from?" I could barely speak. "What proof do you have, Don?"

"I was standing in the entrance hall next to the front door and watched you leave with him," he mouthed.

"Don, that's impossible; you were having a nightmare. Don, you can't stand."

He stared at me for a very long time. I felt the ice of his feelings running through my body. His piercing look made me crumble, and the tears on my face were finding their way down my neck.

How in the world could this be happening to me? I silently begged, *Please, God. God, stop this, I can't bear it. What have I done to deserve this?* The memory of people saying, "God only gives you what you can bear," was repeating over and over in my mind. I hate that expression. If there is a God, and God is good, he wouldn't do such a thing. I never want to hear that expression again, and I'll never say it to anyone.

I had no idea what was going on in Don's mind. I guess he was thinking what any man would be thinking who felt like he was "less of the man" than he was. I could see he'd had a nightmare that was so realistic he believed it was true, but was he starting to understand this, or was he convinced I had been unfaithful? I was devastated and could only hope he was questioning his thoughts and coming to the conclusion that it had been a nightmare. I could see that it had felt so real, was so deep beneath the layers of his imagination, that his struggle was to believe his thoughts or to believe me.

My life had become a roller coaster. It had been eighteen months, and the emotions I was going through were taking a toll on me. I felt like I was walking around a volcano with my toes dangling over the edge. I was being a cheerleader for Don, a pillar of unwavering strength to my family and friends, but the whole time, I was faking it. They all thought I was strong, but inside I was shattered glass and each turn cut me deeper. The cuts pierced me to my core, and I was merely holding on by my fingertips.

The loyal doctors were at their wit's end with me, too, and kept saying, "Kathi, I'm a heart doctor; I'm a neurologist; I can't deal with the enormity of your emotional life. You need to talk to a professional." I was at my breaking point.

One evening, some friends asked me to dinner. I left the house wearing my "I can do it all" face and holding all the feeling of the day within me, but the gravity of it finally came crashing down. I was driving down Sunset Boulevard playing the scene of the morning over and over in my head. The unfairness of it, the months of trying, the sleepless nights. I couldn't take it anymore. I was depressed and completely deprived of a decent night's sleep.

I was staring at the road, not remembering driving from one stretch to another. I was in a trance of sorrow. Not feeling sorry for myself, but a hypnotic state of the last eighteen months swallowing me up. I was staring at the double yellow line. I kept driving, but I thought, *If I went over that double yellow line, my pain would be gone.* I kept thinking it, and there they were in my mind—my beautiful children, and yes, my husband who I loved more than any love I ever thought possible. I grasped the steering wheel tightly and knew I had to go on. I had reached a dangerous depth of depression, and no one knew it was to such a serious degree. I had hidden it better than even I thought I could.

The next day when two doctors were visiting Don, I stood in the hallway talking to them and uncontrollable tears started to flow. I never wanted Don to have the guilt of causing me any kind of pain, so I made sure we were out of earshot. I looked at the doctors, who had for months been recommending I find professional help, and said, "I'm not crazy. I'm only acting crazy. What's the name of the therapist you think I should see?"

"I'm relieved you're going to talk to someone, Kathi." Dr. Liker quickly gave me her name. "No one can possibly go through what you're going through without professional help."

"Will you call and explain my situation?" I was nervous to talk to a stranger about my life and didn't want to spend the first meeting explaining everything. I wanted to get to the nitty gritty.

Dr. Shpiner gave me fantastic advice. He said, "You know what it's like to open a road map and then how hard it is to fold it back? Kathi, you don't need to open the entire map. Only open the part of the map you're dealing with now."

I walked nervously into Dr. Bonnie Berman's office not know-ing what to expect, but I got right to the point and told her how devastated I was at Don's accusations. Dr. Berman understood and respected that mindset, and with that, we were off.

"If Don wasn't ill and treated you like this, what would you do?" she asked.

"I'd probably get really upset," I said, "and strongly, and I mean very strongly, give him a piece of my mind."

"Then why don't you?"

"Are you kidding? He's a quadriplegic on a respirator. How could I even think of raising my voice to him? He's fragile."

"Kathi," Bonnie said evenly. "He has no right to treat you unfairly. You deserve the respect he's always given you. You need to interact with him as you always have. It's your life, too. You've told me you're trying to make life as normal as possible for him; then act normal. It's a two-way street. Do you think Don would be open to meeting me?"

"I doubt it," I told her. "Actually, I would be shocked if he agreed to meet with you."

Don was up in his wheelchair waiting for me to come home. He knew I was going to see a therapist and didn't react to the idea one way or another, but when I walked in the door he was interested in what had happened. I casually mentioned the doctor would like to meet him, and to my utter astonishment he mouthed, "OK."

"When?" I asked, still shocked.

"Today," he answered.

I immediately called Bonnie. "Do you think you could come up to our house today to meet with Don before he changes his mind?" I did not want to lose this opportunity.

"I think I could rearrange some appointments and be at your home as soon as possible," she said.

By the time Bonnie arrived, Don was back in bed. I led her into our room and introduced her to Don. I took a seat next to him, and she sat at the foot of his bed. Within minutes she got right to the point. She asked Don all sorts of questions about how he felt about his manhood. I was shocked he was answering her, "Yes, I do feel less."

"Are you feeling like you can't fulfill Kathi's needs in the same way you did before you were ill?" she asked.

"Yes," he answered. "I can't."

My heart was crushed listening to this conversation. The afternoon was filled with his emotions pouring out through lip-reading and the spelling board. I had never seen this kind of vulnerability from Don, and at the same time, I was in awe watching him convey his deepest feelings to a complete stranger. This was so unlike him. The depth of his hurt must have been unbearable for him to open up like this. I tried to hold back my tears, but it was impossible. Bonnie had him describe his dream, had me use every bit of energy I had left to argue my feelings and not let him get away with how he was treating me.

As I walked her to the door, she stopped and looked me straight in the eyes. "Kathi, I heard your story before I came here, but this is much more complicated than I ever imagined. In the thirty-plus years I have been a therapist, I've seen a lot, but nothing like this. I think you're deeply depressed, and if you'd like me to admit you into a hospital for a week, I will."

"I don't want to go to a hospital. Just knowing that you understand my problems is a beginning I feel like I can work with." I didn't have to see Bonnie too often, but she helped me with the tools I needed to work with my complicated situation. It was constantly a work in progress. Don put me to the test. Through the wringer. I wasn't going to give up, and I could feel it—I had passed his test.

That day, I learned how important professional help is and wished I had sought it sooner. My friends and family had been incredibly supportive, but professionals can be objective where friends and family can't always be.

Friends have your best interest at heart, but they are never walking in your shoes and seldom have any experience with the problem at hand emotionally—or in my case, medically. My friends were very sympathetic, and I don't know what I would have done without them, but in many instances, their advice did not come from experience. It came from their personal opinions. I welcomed all the ideas and suggestions, and many times it helped, but sometimes it was difficult. Medical suggestions would come up—friends excitedly reading about and sharing new solutions and treatments—enthusiasm always came from a good place; but I often ended up feeling guilty that I wasn't putting Don on a plane to wherever the newest possibility was. I appreciated their enthusiasm, but there were some suggestions that I knew were medically and logistically impossible, and I wasn't ready to divulge the deeply personal reasons why. I ran everything by the doctors, but more often than not, I learned the "lay suggestion" had no bearing on Don's case because they had no idea or experience with all its complexities. I could tell it hurt some people's feelings when they felt they were being ignored, but at the end of the day, my steadfast focus was always Don's well-being and happiness.

Seeking a professional helped me deal with these delicate situations. The therapist I found was a much-needed sounding board who helped me develop a skill set that would aid me emotionally through many situations. Someone to talk to who had absolutely no skin in the game, no emotion, no one-sided opinions. I could say things I'd be too embarrassed to share with friends. I could vent my frustrations without feeling I was being judged. It was hugely beneficial for Don to meet with the therapist, too. As I said, I was shocked when he agreed. She immediately got to the heart of subjects I would never have had the nerve to approach, and I quickly learned he wanted to talk about his frustrations. He needed a facilitator to listen, to be a bridge between the two of us. He was a typical guy wanting to "fix" things, not skirt around them. He only met with the therapist once, but that one time was a lifesaver.

Don's vocabulary never included phrases like "no" or "I can't" or "you should have." His optimism was contagious, and luckily I caught it, otherwise my days and nights would have been completely unbearable. The mind is an interesting thing. Controlling it no matter how difficult it can be is a gift, especially when living in an unusual situation.

"Don," I cooed one morning, my face close to his, "Dr. Shpiner is visiting this evening. He won't be in too much of a rush this time, so what do you say we greet him in our living room and make it a nice little casual evening like we do with our friends?"

Don was lying on his side as his nurse was dressing him, listening and staring attentively into my eyes. His morning dressing routine was sometimes the best time for me to capture his full attention. He laid propped up on his side as his nurse rolled him from one side to the other to dress him. I knelt next to him with my chin resting on the mattress and quickly changed to the opposite side when he was turned. These early morning conversations, nose to nose, were a little trick I came up with to distract him and spare his embarrassment of being bathed and dressed by someone other than himself.

I had reconstructed all his pants with Velcro on their sides and his shirts split in the back with soft ribbons. This way he could wear "normal" rather than "handicap" clothes and look as handsome as ever. Before Don's stroke, he never much cared about what outfit I thought he should wear, trusting everything I suggested would coordinate. Now even this task was something he personally and fully embraced, savoring control wherever possible. Each morning I would hold up at least three or four different choices, and as if studying a finely shaded Monet, he made his choice for the day.

"OK," Don mouthed with his genuine, loving smile. "Let's meet Shpiner in the living room tonight."

Looking out past the pool as the sun set over the mountains and peacefully sank into the Pacific, Don and I relaxed in our living room as we awaited Dr. Shpiner's visit. I felt so adult in this room; the gilded clock ticking away on the mantel, exquisitely hand-painted silk cloth upholstered chairs, and the soft grey-blue chenille fabric covering the fringe-trimmed sofa tied it all together. We could have been in a Parisian pied-à-terre or a sophisticated apartment in Rome. No, we were in our own little jewel box in the middle of Los Angeles—the home we created for ourselves decorated with treasures we had collected together. Across the room a fire gently flickered and the amber reflection on Don's face mirrored his contentment, or so I had come to believe.

The bell rang, and I quickly greeted Dr. Shpiner as he walked across our courtyard to the side kitchen door he always used.

"Bob," I called, "this way. Come through the front door. Don is up in his wheelchair waiting for you. You always visit with us so early in the morning. We never have the chance to casually talk and enjoy our time with you." My thoughts momentarily detoured to the time Don and I ran into his dermatologist in Century City on our way to a movie. He had never seen Don up out of bed and was shocked to see how great he looked, albeit in his wheelchair. Dr. Shpiner seemed to have the same reaction as he followed me and spotted Don waiting for him. I pulled up a chair for him to sit close to us, and we began the evening with short pleasantries.

Our time together changed in a matter of minutes. The dark clouds slowly replacing Don's smile were a sure sign a storm was brewing, but it was his eyes that always gave way to his true feelings. He looked straight into Dr. Shpiner's eyes and mouthed, "Will I ever walk again?"

"No," Dr. Shpiner answered without hesitation.

"Will I ever talk again?" he mouthed with precision, wanting to be completely understood.

"No," Dr. Shpiner answered.

"Will I ever breathe again?"

Time ground to a stop as Dr. Shpiner looked straight into Don's eyes, and with conviction said, "No, Don, I am so sorry."

The air was as thick as London fog. I was holding in every raw feeling I had ever possessed. These questions…where had they come from all of a sudden?

Don looked intently into Dr. Shpiner's eyes and mouthed, "Then why should I live?" Turning to me, he mouthed, "I want to go to bed now."

I was devastated, and it was apparent Dr. Shpiner was too. It had been eighteen months since Don's stroke, and our life was finally starting to have a semblance of acceptance. Don had been so convincingly optimistic that he had us all believing he was on a positive track mentally. I hadn't taken into consideration that he wanted to hear the truth. The absolute, unadulterated, brutal truth.

After Don's nurse wheeled him from the living room, my eyes immediately filled with tears that quickly ran down my face. As I wiped the moisture from my cheeks with the sleeve of my blouse, I said, "Dr. Shpiner, Don will be gone by tomorrow. He doesn't want to live anymore."

I quietly crawled into bed next to Don, trying not to wake him. Every nerve in my body hemorrhaged with sadness as I gently put my hand on his chest. It was pulsating to the rhythm and melodic sound of his ventilator. Don knew the truth now.

Very early the next morning, I opened my eyes to the DK Team swirling around us, practically running into one another like a Three Stooges skit. Don was shouting in his own special way, "I want two physical therapies each day instead of one along with speech therapy and whatever else you all think I need."

"What's happening?" Don's nurse asked.

I looked from Don to his nurse and back again, giving the biggest smile I think I had ever had. "Don wants to live. It's a new normal. Let's make it happen."

It was at that moment I realized Don had accepted his life. A mammoth moment important to every patient and to every caregiver. Accepting a new life was the only way I was able to chart the uncertain and compromising waters we were sailing through.

9

RELEARNING TO FLY

"There is a thin line that separates laughter and pain, comedy and tragedy, humor and hurt."
—Erma Bombeck

For years after Don's stroke, I never even considered going away without him. Our world-traveling ways seemed like a distant dream. Being a caregiver was more than a full-time job, and the thought of being absent came with a whole new set of anxieties and complexities.

"Don, I just got off the telephone with Donna and Greg Econn. They've invited me to join them, along with Kimmy and Watty, for five days in the Dominican Republic at a home they've rented. What would you think if I went too?" I nervously asked. I wasn't sure what Don was thinking as he turned his head away from me. He had a pensive look on his face and seconds seemed like minutes. Was he upset with me? Did he realize I hadn't been anywhere for quite a while? Was he worried about being home without me? "Don, I've talked to my kids, your kids, and some of our friends. Everyone is willing to take turns staying here so you won't be alone with just the medical staff. Bryan and Paul volunteered, and they've been here since day one. You'll be in good hands."

He turned back towards me, and with a half-hearted smile mouthed, "Yes, you should go."

I hugged him as best I could while not pulling on his trach. The darn trach and tubes were always in my way, but I knew how to carefully maneuver around them. As he watched tears filling my eyes, I think he realized how much this little trip was going to mean to me. I knew he was being unselfish. That was Don, and even with his challenging life he tried to find ways to give back to me.

It was so hard to leave my children when they were young, but the list of instructions I left for their care paled in comparison to the list I made this time. Our home was finally running like a finely tuned clock, but any changes could throw it completely out of kilter. I couldn't forget a single thing before I left, and those volunteers, or I should say angels, who were to stay with Don needed a lot of advice on how our days operated. Movie days were planned, outings to restaurants, partner meetings, and grandchild swim lessons at the house for Don to watch. My friend Jenny Jones filled many spots on the calendar to read to Don. "Kathi, I thought Don would enjoy a story from the *Wall Street Journal* or *The Economist*. No, he wanted me to read *The National Enquirer* to him," she later shared with me when I returned.

When I was on the plane, I couldn't stop thinking about Don. Friends and family had encouraged me to go, saying I needed to take a little time for myself. I kept having doubts about that advice. I felt terrible without Don. My mind was full of memories. I could smell him and sense him sitting next to me. I could feel us arm-in-arm as we always were when our flights would take off, but he wasn't with me this time. I was thinking about him in his blue cashmere sweater. He always wore that sweater when we traveled. Even though I was with a group of friends, I still felt so lonely without Don. It was impossible not to be scared that something might happen while I was away. Everyone told me that it was good for me, but I had a hard time being apart from Don.

Now, I can look back and understand how important a little time to myself was. It's not easy to leave your loved one, whether you can afford it or not, but little times here and there are vitally important. It's impossible to keep up caregiver energy twenty-four hours a day without falling apart, and falling apart doesn't help anyone, especially the caregiver.

I was fortunate to have the resources to travel, but learned very quickly that being away for more than a few days was harder than I could imagine. It was very difficult on Don, too. He would practically close his eyes the entire time I was gone, hoping sleep would make the time apart go quicker. I, on the other hand, would think of Don the entire time I was gone. Wherever I was, he was constantly on my mind; sometimes I felt like I might as well have stayed home. I was miserable. After a few days I would adjust a bit and take the time to try to feel free of problems and imagine I was living the life we lived before Don became ill. My imagination was never completely successful. The saddest part was returning to a life I had unrealistically dreamed would be fixed when I walked through the front door. It was far from it.

With a few flight changes behind us, we finally reached our destination. I had no idea what to expect, but I quickly got the sense that the Dominican Republic was going to be laid back and casual, like Cabo. As the five of us drove up to the house, I felt like Cinderella arriving at the ball. My problems were behind me, but only physically. Emotionally I had a pit in my stomach. The house was beautiful and the Econns gave me the best room right on the sea. Everyone was doing their part to make me feel included, but I'm sure they sensed how difficult the journey was for me.

We started the week by playing tennis sets. It reminded me of the times Don and I were in St. Tropez, and he'd come along with me to watch me play matches at a neighbor's home. "Don, this is just a little social neighborhood thing. You're not supposed to clap and make such a big deal every time I make a point. It's getting a little embarrassing," I'd say to him as my partner and I switched sides. I needed him back. I needed to hear his cheers. I could hardly hit the ball.

As the sun was setting that evening, we were still sitting by the pool looking out over the Caribbean as Frank Sinatra came on the stereo. My mind drifted to the times Don and I lounged on our chaises in Cabo, listening to music under clear star-studded skies. Memories of our first evening together in our Beverly Hills home filled my thoughts, too. The evening was balmy, the living room pocket door windows were completely open to the outside. I was wearing my long slinky nightgown. He took me in his arms, twirled me around, and we danced all around the pool till we fell onto the sofa where our romantic evening…I wanted those days back again.

The Dominican Republic was a wonderful escape for me, especially with the pampering from my friends. I was having fun, but how could I be? I felt guilty enjoying myself, knowing Don was struggling at home. My days were a reprieve from the endless responsibilities so very far away, but a minute didn't go by that I didn't think about my real life.

Guilt is the number-one word I hear from caregivers over and over again. It was the feeling I never escaped. He was ill. I wasn't. He couldn't talk. I could. He couldn't walk. I could. He couldn't control his life. I could. I was happy I went to the movies today. He wasn't. I was happy to take a break. He was lonely when I was gone. "How perfect can I be?" I'd question. The list went on and on.

I would've loved to see Don handle our island outing. We signed up for a boat to take us snorkeling, but the boat turned out to be one with a cast of thousands. Can you just picture it? Scuba tanks hanging off the side, tourists (like we weren't?), lots and lots of people. We decided to charter our own boat, which turned out to be a great idea.

We motored to an island that was pretty, but nothing like the places Don took me to. It made me think about our trip to Corsica and some of the little beaches we went to. "This week is your time to not have anything on your mind," the group would repeat. It was so nice to hear, but I couldn't sit still because, when I did, I couldn't get Don off my mind. I thought about him all day long—almost every minute.

We ended the day back at the house resting by the pool and playing dominoes for hours. The best part was never having to change out of our bathing suits. Now this is what I call luxury. Little did I know that we were in for more adventure and luxury than we'd expected.

"Hey, Greg, you want to go for a golf cart ride?" I asked one of my hosts near the end of the week. "I have an idea."

In he jumped, and off we went. I had received an email from my friend Mary Ourisman, who heard I was in the Dominican Republic, saying she was at Casa Grande, and her hostess would love to see me. Greg and I made our way to Casa Grande and found what we thought was a hotel. We arrived at the same time as a crew that was setting up for a party that evening. No one—guards and all—realized we didn't belong. The guards just thought we were part of the guest list. We drove through the open gates down a long, winding driveway shaded by magnificent trees arching over the road. We knocked on what we thought was the entrance door. Slowly I turned the knob as Greg and I looked at each other with wide eyes.

"Why not?" Greg shrugged.

"Hello? Hello. Anyone home?" I shouted. There was no answer. I'd been friends with Greg since high school and knew he'd be up for a little mischief.

Slowly we entered. Where was the reception desk? Where were all the people? It soon became clear we were not in a hotel. We were trespassing in someone's home. With nervous energy, we took our own private tour. My heart was racing. I hadn't done such a brazen thing since fifth grade when my friends and I climbed over the wall of silent screen star Harold Lloyd's home in Bel Air. Although an armed guard quickly chased us out, we caught a glimpse of the private play yard—an exact replica of a Cotswold village—and a zoo with monkeys in a large ornate cage. "We need to be friends with this kid," I said to my friends.

Greg and I explored room after room, each more beautiful than the last. We even took photos of each other on the veranda overlooking the sea. Were we crazy? As our confidence grew, we began exploring the grounds. We turned a corner, and before we could run, we came upon a woman sitting alone by the pool.

"Are you Kathi Koll?" she asked. Greg and I were blown away.

"Yes." We were caught. And she knew my name.

"I'm so glad you found me. I'm Lucy, and my hostess would like to invite you and your guests for lunch tomorrow."

"We'd love to come," I quickly answered. We were still surprised she wasn't even the least bit suspicious of how we had ended up on the pool deck in front of her. It was a successful adventure, and the next day we all spent with our new friends was as grand as Casa Grande.

My week seemed long, but by the time it ended, I realized how quickly it really flew by. I was getting anxious towards the end and missed Don more than ever. The plane ride home seemed never-ending. As I looked out the plane's window to the beautiful land and sea below, I closed my eyes and thought about what Don said to me right before we got married: "I'm worried about our age difference. You might be left alone one day."

"It doesn't matter. A few years with you would be better than no years at all."

Now I understand what he meant. But even though our time was cut short, it is more special than I will ever be able to explain to anyone. I wish we could have held on to what we had, but I have our memories—our life together and dreams that really did come true. Of course, I wish I could change how difficult our journey was, but in many ways I wouldn't change it for the world. Don taught me how precious life is and how special it is to be in love. For that I will be eternally grateful.

I couldn't wait to see Don. When I entered the house, I dropped my bags at the front door and ran down the hall with lightning speed. I couldn't get to him fast enough. I burst into our room full of excitement. Don's beautiful smile was waiting for me, but the incredible joy I thought I'd feel quickly faded. It felt like a ton of bricks had just fallen on me. My situation, his situation, the world's situation, it all looked bleaker than ever. I was so happy to see him, but nothing was fixed; he was still paralyzed, was still on a ventilator. He looked so fragile. His color was different. He looked older and weaker than my memory of him. I felt like I was starting all over again. I struggled to put a smile on my face. My heart was heavy, and I was fighting back tears. He was still so sick. I wanted my husband back. The one I married. The one who took care of me. My best friend and life partner. Where was he?

That trip taught me a lot about being a caregiver. Breaks can do a world of good for caregivers and patients, but my trip to the Dominican Republic was too long. With small breaks—a day here, a day there—I didn't leave my life emotionally. I was able to step back in without sadness but with a refreshed outlook and a renewed strength. Patients can become selfish and not realize how hard the caregiver has it when it's always about the patient, never the caregiver. Don appreciated me more when I came home. My break wasn't unbearable for him, but it did give him a chance to think about what I did for him. His loneliness gave him the time to sit back and clearly look at the value I was giving to him in his life, both physically and emotionally. There was a lot more "I love you" and "thank you," which was all I really needed. Those words gave me the strength to do my job as a caregiver, but with a refreshed peace of mind.

I knew that this break would help move our relationship forward, both as a couple and as teammates in our new normal, and make us better able to tackle whatever came our way. With hindsight 20/20, I see the things I'd do differently that first time away, but those mistakes were also part of what kept us on track and prepared us for the future. We each got to reevaluate our priorities and how best to manifest those in our lives.

The most important thing to Don was to walk again. I thought his first choice would be talking, but he was bent on walking. Not one physical therapy session a day, but two. Don took his therapy very seriously, so it was important that his therapist be a good match for him. I never knew why, but one particular therapist drove him crazy, so she had to go. She retaliated by egging everyone's cars—including the doctors'. It couldn't be proven, nor did I have the time or energy to confront her, but everyone knew it wasn't just neighborhood hooligans. I was living with so many people I barely knew. People I liked. People I didn't. It was its own little world, and sometimes I felt like I would drown in it.

Don worked so incredibly hard on his various therapies, and it was exhausting for him. In between sessions, he took long naps. There was no possible way he could have visitors during the day. He insisted that if anyone wanted to visit, it had to be after 4:00 PM because he was working. He didn't want anything or anyone to get in the way of his way of recovery. Some of his family members expressed disappointment in this choice, because they didn't want to drive from Newport Beach to Los Angeles during traffic hours. Because the messenger always gets killed, I took a lot of heat for it; but those were Don's rules, and I made it clear this was Don's time and not time for anyone else's convenience. In his mind, it was no different than working at the office or being in a meeting.

Along with physical and occupational therapy, he had speech therapy most days to get any possible chance of voice out of him and keep his vocal cords exercised. I never realized how important getting his jaw moving was until I witnessed Don suffer lockjaw at one point. It was very dangerous because if he had to be intubated for any reason, it would be impossible to get a tube down his throat. Even with speech therapy and mouth exercises, he experienced it from time to time. The only solution was injections of Botox administered into his jaw to enable it to move freely. Over the years, I used to joke with him that he must be asking for extra shots because he looked awfully good.

On top of it all, he was running his business. His partners came to the house a few times a week, and in between, they emailed reports that I read to Don.

"Do you want me to reread this to you?" I'd ask after reading a long, boring email. I thought there was a lot of complicated information, and he might not understand it completely just from my oral reading. I certainly needed more time to understand it in between my gulps of water.

"No, don't stop," he'd mouth. "Read more." He got it all and was very impatient. I couldn't read fast enough for how quickly he picked it all up.

Don's career was a large part of his life. As soon as he could communicate with me, he told me he wanted me at the office every day. He wanted to know exactly what was going on and wanted me to understand the business. One of the last things he said to Jerry, his son-in-law and colleague, on his way to the hospital the day of his stroke was, "If anything happens to me, are you prepared to work with Kathi?" Jerry assured him he was.

It might be serendipity, but a year or so before Don's stroke, he asked me to work with him on a development he was about to start in Cabo. He knew I had built spec homes—an 'If you build it, they will come' style endeavor—when I lived in Missouri and was impressed at what a tight ship I ran on a rather complicated home we built together in Mexico. Even before we were married, I had built spec homes in Mexico, and I was always excited to get involved in projects there. I had done some limited work with him on a proposed project on Catalina Island, but Cabo was going to be different. It was the project we both had our hearts set on. His company was running smoothly; he had a good team, and this was going to be the project we could have fun with and do together.

It was a time in his life when he could have retired, but that was never something Don would do. "Some of the guys from Stanford University used to be so interesting for me to talk to when they were still working," he said after a reunion once. "We'd discuss the world, our careers, and our futures. Now when I ask them what they're doing, they say, 'Well, I get up in the morning and have breakfast with my wife, then I go to the golf course, then I play gin with the guys, then I go home and have a cocktail with my wife, then we have dinner, then I go to sleep.' They do the same thing every day. I'll never retire."

As soon as the purchase of the Hacienda property closed, Don had the two of us working on plans with the architectural firm Hart Howerton in San Francisco. Everywhere Don and I went, every vacation we took, the project was on our mind. We'd be walking down a beach in Sardinia and spot a stone wall—"Perfect for the entrance," we'd agree—or be having a massage in Bali—"The size of the treatment rooms should be a little bigger." We were constantly on the phone with the architects behind the scenes chuckling at the hours we called. Morning: serious call. Late afternoon San Francisco time: "OK, guys, they're calling from St. Tropez after dinner. Get ready for some creative ideas." The rosé always made us more imaginative. We were designing a dream project together, and at the same time, having the time of our life. It was a wonderful collaboration resulting in a first-class resort. Sadly, once construction started, I had to spearhead the efforts without Don because of his illness.

Land's End, at the tip of Baja California, Mexico, was merely the small fishing village of Cabo San Lucas and scarcely inhabited when Bud Parr, a contractor from California, and Luis Coppola, who'd been a US Air Force pilot, arrived in 1947. Rod Rodriguez, the son of a former president of Mexico, built the small forty-eight-room Palmilla Hotel in 1956 near neighboring San Jose del Cabo as a fishing refuge for luminaries such as Bing Crosby, John Wayne, and Desi Arnaz. Funny to think so many years later his daughter, Lucie, would be my best childhood friend. Bud Parr, his nemesis, built the only other hotels in the area, the Hotel Cabo San Lucas in 1961 and, in 1963, the Hacienda Hotel located at the tip of Baja in the almost-nonexistent town of Cabo San Lucas. Coppola was responsible for the Finisterra in 1972. These three men were the true pioneers of Cabo starting in the early '50s.

When Don appeared on the scene in 1964, not much had changed. He was a young man with curiosity, an enviable zest for life, ambition that saw no boundaries, and an idea of turning this sleepy little fishing village into something, but at the time, he didn't know what. He had met a bush pilot who recommended that Don fly his small plane down the coast of Baja. When Don reached Land's End, he circled over the famous arch and spotted the Hacienda Hotel, which was the only building for miles. In those days, there was no town of Cabo San Lucas, just San Jose del Cabo, the historical town twenty miles north. Don landed his plane on a dirt runway in a dried-up riverbed, which is now a large marina holding thousands of boats. He walked up the beach, explored around the hotel, and decided he wanted to own it one day. He explored the rest of the area, but in those days there was only a narrow, arduous road connecting the resorts, which made driving prohibitively difficult. Each hotel had a small dirt airstrip on which to land. Don had no idea his dreams would turn into what Cabo is today.

He was the second wave, and what a tidal wave he created. Don took what Rod and Bud built and brought the area into a whole new world. The world of golf. The world of first-class resorts. Don never wanted to do anything half-assed, as he would say, and knew for Cabo to flourish, golf and hotels had to be first class.

"Who's the best golf designer in the world?" he asked someone at his office.

The answer came back, "Jack Nicklaus."

"Then let's hire him," he said enthusiastically.

As he worked tirelessly on the project, his friends would say, "Don, I hope you're not putting any of your own money into Cabo; it'll never work. Cabo is a world-class fishing mecca," they'd prod, "but no one goes there to play golf."

Don's gut told him something different. He shook off their barbs, and with the help of Jack's keen eye for course design, propelled Cabo into the world-famous golf resort it is now. Building Cabo del Sol was a creative labor of love for Don, and the course was quickly ranked in the top 100 of the world by *Golf Digest*. Today, there are as many golf bags as fishing rods arriving at the airport.

Don was on a roll and loving it. He bought the Palmilla Hotel in 1984 along with the surrounding beachfront and hillside, added another hundred rooms to it, built the Palmilla Jack Nicklaus Signature Golf Course, had the highway moved, and developed the adjoining land into private home sites. He then mirrored his efforts at Cabo del Sol, a five-mile stretch nestled south in a beautiful cove along the Sea of Cortez. The owner was Bud Parr. When Don showed up with cash in hand to settle their deal, Bud sat on the other side of his desk and said, "I've changed my mind about the price. And I always get my way."

He pulled a cloth off his desk, revealing—in true Wild West fashion—a loaded gun facing right at Don. Don leaped towards him and said, "Bud, if you don't take that gun right now and put it in the bottom drawer of your desk, I'm going to take it, stick it up your ass, and shoot your flipping brains out!" (and flipping is not the word he used). Surprised, Bud followed orders, and they made their deal. Don's charisma was a big part of his reputation, but it didn't take long for people to realize he shouldn't be crossed.

Forty years later, Don said to me, "Come on, Kathi, get in the car. We're going to the Hacienda to talk to Mark Parr." He was one of the three sons who inherited the resort from their infamous father, Bud. I loved listening to Don come up with a strategy for how the conversation would go and the rapport we'd develop with Mark. "OK, Kathi, don't talk too much, and don't talk too little," he coached as we drove down the coast. "You grew up near Mark, right? Talk about your old neighborhood."

We played this game for two years before he made his deal. It took a lot of negotiations, dinners, and lunches to get there, but what an experience it was for me. The education I received watching Don was priceless, and I enjoyed every minute of it. None of this came without guts, sheer determination, and his insatiable love for the area. Many say Don put Cabo on the map. He paved the way for the third wave, those landing their private Gulfstream jets today, bragging to their friends about the new unspoiled resort destination of Cabo they've "discovered."

Mark knew Don could be trusted and didn't want the property to go to anyone else. Don had earned a stellar reputation in Cabo. He loved Cabo and Cabo loved him. Don was respected and loved by the local people of Cabo, because his resorts and developments were responsible for the creation of thousands of jobs. He was honored for his generosity towards the community in 2006 when Governor Narcisco Agúndez named the new fifty-two-acre sports complex The Don Koll Sports Center, an unheard of honor for a "gringo" in Cabo.

Don measured success by a very simple yardstick. For our fifth anniversary, we flew to a resort on mainland Mexico. As we landed our small plane, Don said, "This place isn't doing very well. Look at the iron. We have the best plane here." We returned to Cabo after our anniversary weekend, and he said, "Look how great Cabo is doing! We have the shittiest little plane here." Seeing the prosperity of Cabo gave him more pleasure than anything he personally gained from it.

I visited the construction site of the sports center with Don many times during its early stages. He always took pleasure in watching the work being done and the excitement it was bringing to local people involved—especially our good friend Marco Ehrenberg, who had spent countless hours working to make this dream come true.

When I think of Don's and my new normal, one of the most challenging and important pieces was how to get Don back to Cabo San Lucas, Mexico, the city he held deep within his heart. Standing at the foot of our bed, watching Dr. Shpiner about to perform an emergency trach change, I looked at Don and said, "Don, tomorrow's Valentine's Day, and I promise you, we will be in Cabo next year on Valentine's Day."

Dr. Shpiner looked up and said, "What are you talking about?"

"We have a year to figure it out," I answered. "Let's make it happen."

When I shared my idea with Dr. Shpiner and a few others again months later, it once again fell upon deaf ears. "There's no way you can take a completely paralyzed man on a respirator 1,500 miles south to Mexico," the doctor said.

Then Marco called me one afternoon and said, "The governor wants to have an opening ceremony for the community, and he's hoping Don can make it."

With Don's fragile condition we could never commit 100%, but we explained to all concerned how excited he was and that he would do his best to make it. The governor was even generous enough to open the schedule to any day or time of day that would be convenient for Don.

I really didn't think it would be anything other than a few dignitaries. If I had known what the event was really going to be like, I would have had all our family and friends there. When the event rolled around, though, we were glad to have three couples visiting us who were excited to come along. As we left the house, me in the van with Don and our friends following in another car, we were stopped by a police officer waiting for us to exit our driveway. He was there to escort us to the ceremony. We drove down the highway with a line of police cars—red lights and sirens leading the way.

As we turned off the highway and followed the escort through the local community near Cabo San Lucas, which is now a city of thousands, the road turned to dirt and was full of potholes. We had to hold Don's head tightly in place against the wheelchair headrest, for fear it'd fall forward and he'd be injured. But he didn't mind; he was smiling ear to ear. The energy changed from a tourist town to a local community brimming with excitement. There were banners on every corner.

"Look, Don," I said. "Look over there at that sign. It says, 'THANK YOU DON KOLL!' Look at that one. It says, 'BIENVENIDO DON KOLL.'" There were people everywhere making their way to the sports center. Families pushing baby strollers. Dogs running down the street. Teenagers laughing with their friends. Older people slowly maneuvering through the throngs of attendees. Police directing traffic. It was amazing. We arrived at the stadium where the unfinished parking lot was full of cars, busses, bicycles, and people. As we approached, hundreds of people made way for us to drive to a little spot next to an ambulance. The organizers had thought of everything.

"Hi, everyone," said our friend Marco as he came up to the van. "There's going to be several activities, and then, Kathi, you'll speak for Don."

"Marco, are you kidding me? I'm giving a speech?" I was shocked.

"Don't worry, Kathi," he said. "You'll be great, and I have an interpreter for you since you don't speak Spanish."

One of our friends chimed in, "I thought we were going to a little gymnasium somewhere. What in the heck is going on?"

Marco escorted us to an area in the outside arena where the governor greeted us. Through his interpreter, he asked if there was any way Don would have the stamina to circle the stadium with him. I asked Don what he thought, and he mouthed, "Absolutely."

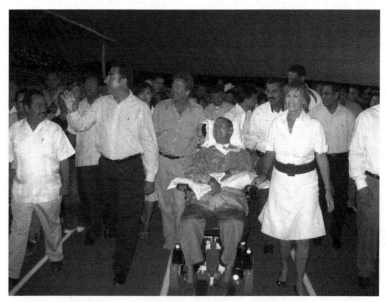

Opening ceremeony at Estadio Don Koll with
Governor Narciso Agúndez Montaño

We took our position alongside the governor in the front of about fifty dignitaries, local businessmen, senators, and city council members. You name them—they were there. To open the ceremony, the local high school band paraded onto the field followed by a group of drum majorettes. A number of grade-school soccer teams represented in different colored uniforms lined the track as we started the procession, with me operating Don's wheelchair. There were thousands of people filling the stands, and those who didn't have a seat were lined five deep outside a fence. As we passed by the crowd seated in the bleachers, they stood in a wave motion and chanted, "DON KOLL, DON KOLL." The only dry eyes in the house were Don's as he flashed his wide smile to everyone from the top of the bleachers to those peering through the chain-link.

When it was my turn to speak, I looked at the crowd and shared with them the story of when and why Don first ventured to Cabo, starting with, "When my husband first arrived here in 1964 by way of his small plane, most of you hadn't even been born." I shared his love for the area and respect for the people. I finished my speech with, "Don is an American who loves his country, but a huge part of his heart lies here and always will." The sky lit up with fireworks along with endless cheering and applause. Families lined up to introduce themselves to Don and posed to have their children's pictures taken with him. It was an unforgettable experience for me, and the smile it brought to Don's face showed not only his joy, but also the deep gratitude for the country he loved and respected.

* * *

During the first eighteen months, I still clung to the idea he'd get better. Dr. Shpiner told me too much time had passed, and Don would never get off the respirator and breathe on his own. Each time the doctor visited, I'd follow him out of the house to his car and say,

"Haven't you ever seen the *Guinness Book of World Records*? Don's going to be in it. He's going to get off the respirator."

Between the regular medical staff, medical specialists, therapists, someone to cut Don's hair and clip, his nails there were a multitude of different people coming and going throughout the year. I normally did Don's nails, but sometimes he'd get a real manicure and pedicure, which was imperative. Some people worked regular shifts, some would only come once or twice a month, but all had to be scheduled.

The job was daunting, but after a while, it became routine. The part that never settled into regularity was Don's fragile condition. It could change within minutes. He could go from being stable to having a temperature of 101 and spiking in an instant. His personality could change from happy to depressed in a matter of moments. The dreaded unknown was always lurking. Even seemingly banal things like sleeping position became important, scheduled parts of life. His skin specialist came to educate us on the fragility of skin in Don's condition. She explained that skin breakdown could lead to bedsores, which could easily become complicated by infection. "Many people don't realize it, but bedsores were the source of Christopher Reeves' problems in the end," she informed us before explaining the complex schedule of turning and repositioning Don would need every two hours, twenty-four hours a day.

"You know, Kathi," Don's long-time doctor, John Storch, said to me once, "your situation is the hardest. There's no beginning and no known end. If Don had a terminal illness, there would be somewhat of a timeframe, but your life is the unknown. Don's life could be a matter of minutes or many years."

He was so right. Every night when I closed my eyes, I had no idea if he'd still be with me in the morning. Every morning as I readied for the day, I never knew if he'd still be with me by nightfall. The uncertainty never escaped me. I later learned that this is called "anticipated grief," a very difficult existence many caregivers live with.

Each night when I kissed Don good night, I'd rest my lips on his cheek. I'd be so close that I couldn't see all the tubes and machines keeping him alive. I'd close my eyes and pretend all was just like it always had been. I'd open my eyes in the morning still nuzzled up against him thinking the same thoughts. Only the reality of the day stole these precious memories.

When the long-term team was pulled together, I did start to get used to having all sorts of people I barely knew living with me. They were the ones Don and I felt most comfortable with. Everyone tried to give me space, but it was impossible to do so. I lived in the same room as Don, and he wanted me by his side as much as possible. I never had a full night's sleep because I awakened every two hours to help turn him. There were always questions, stories, concerns, and problems from the medical staff. One day I timed how long it took me to get from my bedroom to the kitchen and back again for a pencil. Forty-five minutes. I had absolutely no privacy or alone time. Of course, neither did Don.

If I had it to do all over again, knowing what I do now, I'd make a point of carving out time in the day for myself, and now I counsel family caregivers to do the same. No one knows or can easily handle the stress put on a caregiver. As time goes on, the patient becomes increasingly needy and, I hate to say it, selfish. A regular schedule for me would have helped us both. If I had set aside an hour each day on a regular basis, Don would have been used to it and known it was my personal time.

I learned that our medical ward, with so many personalities to live with, was a world unto itself with similar problems to that of a little country. I loved some staff that Don didn't want anything to do with, and he insisted I ask them to leave. "Don't take it personally if you don't work out with Don," I explained to released staff members. "He asked me to marry him without thinking he'd be with me twenty-four hours a day. You're new to him, and he just might not want to spend the rest of his life with you. Good care is one thing, but there has to be a personality fit in a situation like his and mine."

Don wanted one woman gone from the start. Her personality was erratic, but she worked hard to make herself indispensable. As time went on, we felt that her personality swings were suspicious. Even scarier was the realization that many of Don's close emergencies and equipment failures were on her watch. It began to look as if the close calls were constructed. We were in agreement: She had to go, and go quickly. It was a difficult situation that I didn't have the energy to confront head on, but I was dealing with Don's precious life and happiness. My gut instinct is usually right, and in this case, it reminded me that where there's smoke, there's fire. Since Don could never be left alone, I worked with a few trusted nurses, and we worked out a secret backup calendar, which made the transition seamless.

Most of the staff members were dreams come true, and we had a good working relationship. They came to form a bond with Don, and I could tell he felt the same way towards them. It was obvious who he respected and felt secure with, and for the most part, many of the original team were with us till the end. As incredible as the staff was, there were some serious problems in our little world. One heartbreaking situation stood out against all the rest.

Don mouthed to me that he wanted one of the girls fired. I thought she was fantastic. He became extremely upset and was mouthing words so fast I couldn't keep up.

"Slow down," I said. "It can't be that bad."

"Yes it is," Don mouthed, "One of the girls is touching me inappropriately."

Stupidly I said, "Normally you'd call this a hall pass. You wouldn't believe how lucky you were."

He didn't think it was funny at all, and I felt horrible I had kidded him.

"Are you sure?" I asked. "Don, the staff needs to bathe you, and that part of you is part of it."

"I know the difference," he mouthed. If he could have talked, his voice would have been booming. "FIRE HER."

Hearing this confession broke my heart. I felt guilty I didn't know sooner, but how could I have?

10

ONE MORE ROLL IN THE HAY

"Being deeply loved by someone gives you strength,
while loving someone deeply gives you courage."
—Lao Tzu

The first time Mother Dolores came back to Los Angeles from the Abbey was in 2007 when she was invited to be the honorary chair of a Neuropathy event. The Reverend Mother allowed her to attend, knowing it was for a good cause, and I think the rules of the Abbey had lightened up a bit. The evening was filled with the excitement of friends old and new there to welcome Mother Dolores back after so many years being away. My family was there to support my brother and to meet Mother Dolores for the first time. The aunt they almost had. Maria Cooper, Gary Cooper's daughter, was there. She was a childhood friend of my brother's and close to Dolores, along with being another girlfriend of my brother's whom I looked up to as a child. The audience was filled with celebrities excited to welcome Dolores back into their fold.

The first time I met Academy Award–winning actress Patricia Neal, I was visiting Mother Dolores at the Abbey when I was a little girl. The second time our paths crossed was this evening, when I spoke with her about my husband's stroke in hopes that she might have some valuable advice to pass along to me. The stroke she had sustained was legendary, and there had been many articles written about her bravery and strength in fighting back to live a fulfilled life. I was looking for some encouragement, but all she could say was, "Oh dear, my stroke wasn't nearly that bad. I'm so sorry." Several years after Don's death, I watched the Stephen Hawking movie *The Theory of Everything* and wished that Don had been able to operate his wheelchair and speak, even if he remained difficult to understand. Don's physical limitations made his life difficult in ways that made Hawking's look enviable. It would've made a world of difference, but we managed a full, vibrant life regardless.

Dolores was only in town for two days, but she made it very clear to my brother that the two things she wanted to do were meet my husband, whom she and the other sisters had been praying for, and attend the Neuropathy benefit. Before arriving at our home, my brother quietly took Mother Dolores to all their special places, including lunch at the Beverly Hills Hotel. I told my husband how important it was to her to meet him and wondered what he would think of her wanting to spend time with him.

"What do you think?" I asked.

He looked at me with the cutest expression and rolled his eyes as if to say, "Oh brother, what are you getting me into now, Kathi?"

It had been years since my childhood visit to the Abbey, and I was nervous to see Mother Dolores again. I wasn't sure how I was to act or how she would react to me. I had grown up believing she was bigger than life, a movie star with amazing stories. After their wedding was canceled, I thought of the hurt I felt she had caused my brother, the confusion of why she would be in such a place, the wonder of how it would be to greet her as an adult and not as a child. Most of all, I was nervous to see my brother with her. My mind was full of questions of how she could have done this to him. She came in with my brother and another nun, Mother Angele, who was my brother's goddaughter.

We hugged, and she immediately put me at ease. She was the same Dolores from my childhood. Still beautiful with those mesmerizing blue eyes, quick wit, and engaging personality. She didn't seem like a nun at all. She was adorable. Not that nuns can't be adorable, but she just seemed so normal. I don't know what her hair was like because she was in a full habit, and only her face and hands were visible. I don't know exactly what I was expecting, but I guess I thought she'd be serious, pious, and terrifying to me. Her warmth filled the room the minute she walked in. My husband, Don, was waiting for her in the living room, sitting in his wheelchair looking straight ahead. He looked handsome despite his disability, dressed in grey slacks, shirt, and sweater. I refused to buy handicap clothes for him and remodeled his favorite things to accommodate dressing him with ease. They were tailored to open in the back and had Velcro down the sides.

Mother Dolores became very quiet and took a spot close to him. I couldn't hear all the things she was whispering into his ear, but I could see from his face that she was bringing him great comfort. Since he was unable to speak on account of his respirator and his diaphragm being too weak to work even with a Passy Muir valve, I read his lips and interpreted his questions and the conversation back and forth between the two of them. I overheard what Mother Dolores whispered into his ear before she left, "Love doesn't always end at the altar." She said a few prayers and kissed my husband on his forehand, which brought a soothing smile to his face.

When we were alone, fresh with the memory of her visit, I asked him what he thought of her. There was no eye rolling. He looked at me with a quiet sensitivity and mouthed, "She's quite a woman."

Now living in our new normal, I was finding the challenge of keeping Don happy was also keeping me happy. Every time I had an opportunity to do something out of the ordinary, no matter what it was, I went for it.

One evening at a dinner party in Los Angeles, I sat next to a gentleman who mentioned that President Bush, who had only been out of office a month or so, was going to be in Orange County in a couple of days.

"Well," I casually said, "if you have the chance to talk to him, please pass on that if he has five extra minutes and would like to come by the house to say hi to Don, that would be wonderful."

The next thing you know, I receive a call, "President Bush would like to know if you really meant what you said. Can he come by and visit Don?"

"Only if it can be a surprise."

Of course I wouldn't have turned him down if it hadn't been, but the thought of a surprise was so much more fun. The plans were quickly put into motion. Within the hour, my home was being swept by the Secret Service. Keeping them out of Don's view was a challenge in itself. I said to one of the men, "When you go into our room, my husband is going to get suspicious that a strange man in a suit is here. Can you take off your jacket and tie, and I'll tell him you're from the air-conditioning company to check out our system?"

"How are you going to explain my gun?" He had a point.

* * *

Excitement was building as the visit was quickly upon us. I told Don that an old friend was coming by to say hi and asked him to guess who it was going to be. The guessing game was fun in itself, and I knew there was no way in a million years he'd guess President Bush.

The big moment suddenly arrived. Don was settled in our family room ready to greet his "old friend." The Secret Service were out of his view but were signaling me through the window how far the president was. Fifteen minutes. Ten minutes. Eight minutes. Our home is on the water on a small island. The front door is on a side street, but the Secret Service felt the safest way for the president to arrive was by the alley. The president was coming to my house, and rather than arriving by way of the front garden with my beautiful roses, he was going to arrive beside the trash cans.

One of the Secret Service men gave me a three-minute signal.

"I think I heard the doorbell," I said to Don, "I'll be right back with your guest."

I stood in the alley with a number of agents, the rest surrounding our house, not knowing what to expect. All of a sudden a line of motorcycles turned the corner from the street adjacent to the alley. Cycle after cycle, then police car after police car, then a black Suburban that stopped a few feet from me, followed by another Suburban and more police cars and motorcycles. My heart was pounding. *Will he know who I am?* I was thinking. *Of course he will*, I quickly thought. *He's coming to my house, for Christ's sake.*

The president quickly jumped out of the car, gave me a hug, and said, "How's he doing? Is it still a surprise?"

"Yes," I answered nervously. "He has no idea who is coming, the only other time I've surprised him was when I got Cindy Crawford to come over." The president immediately said, "Oh no, Cindy Crawford? He's not going to want to see me."

The president walked into our home, and as he walked from behind Don, he put his hand on Don's shoulder and said, "Hi, buddy, how ya doing?"

Don quickly mouthed, "Great, how are you doing?"

For a second it passed through my mind that Don might think I had paid an impostor and wouldn't believe he was really President Bush. The president sat down in front of Don and instead of staying the agreed five minutes, he stayed for forty-five. I was amazed how easily the conversation flowed back and forth.

I finally asked the president, "How do you know what Don's saying?"

"I can read his lips," he answered.

"Oh boy, you're not leaving. You just found yourself a new job," I laughed.

Daughter Jennifer, son Kevin, George W. Bush, Don, Kathi, daughter-in-law Melissa, and daughter Brooke

As the president was in our home, news quickly spread throughout our neighborhood that something big was going on at the Koll house. As President Bush left, there were close to two hundred neighbors in the alley behind the Secret Service cheering him on. The president had a big smile on his face, and just as quickly as he had arrived, he was gone. I walked back into the house to find Don grinning from ear to ear.

He mouthed, "Where in the world did you find him?"

While I loved big surprises that I knew would make Don's day, they were still special occasions and not the normal everyday routine. I still wanted to maintain the quiet, private moments, too, which required a lot of creativity with all the staff we needed to manage Don's medical requirements.

Tears welled up in my eyes with the memories of our little rituals from before. I loved our evenings when Don would sit on the edge of our tub, and together we would share our day as I relaxed in the warm water of the tub kittishly covered with bubbles. Sometimes we talked and talked and talked. Sometimes he slipped in. I wanted one more chance to have that easy, low-key evening. Please God. Why not? *Yes, we can do it again,* I thought. *But what if he rejected my new crazy idea? Will I feel stupid, weird, creepy?* The what-ifs were a constant and often unwelcome companion in our lives.

"Don, how about taking a bubble bath with me tonight?" I whispered in his ear. His smell and the touch of his skin against the tip of my nose still sent me into a little tizzy.

It was strange how embarrassed I felt asking him this, but life was so different now, and the thought of being naked in front of him was making me feel very uncomfortable. It had been a long time. *He's my husband, for Christ's sake*, I reasoned, trying to convince myself it was normal even though it felt oh so weird. Of course, he was game. He was always game. Life didn't stop being an adventure for him, and my ideas were still his amusement.

The nurses had become part of my family, which helped with my lack of privacy. I did get a little bit of a kick out of the fact that no one seemed surprised with this new idea of mine. Anna, one of the respiratory therapists didn't give a second thought about it and changed Don's tube to an extra-long one that would stretch from the side of our tub, under the door, and into our bedroom where his machine stood next to our bed. Getting through the door was another matter. I could operate his wheelchair with the skill of a concert violinist, but there wasn't a half-inch to spare to get him through the opening. If it didn't work, I was ready to tear out the doorframe.

OK, the scene wasn't quite as it used to be, but I had my husband all alone again in my private little sanctuary. I talked and talked and talked. He didn't take his eyes off of me as he eased my embarrassment with the charm of his schoolboy smile. I don't think he cared what I was talking about. He just seemed happy I had reinvented this sacred part of our relationship.

Even in our own little world, I was still unsure of letting Don see me, but I stood up, arms stretched out as bubbles slid down my side. My added little hip movement brought a big smile to the surprised look on Don's face.

"What do you think?" I asked with all the guts I could muster.

I could almost hear him purr as he mouthed, "I love you."

"Do you think I've gained any weight?" I stupidly asked.

The slight hesitation before his answer was louder than an announcer at Dodger Stadium.

"Yes," he mouthed.

"How many pounds?" *What a dumb question,* I immediately thought.

"Fifteen."

I mustn't have heard him right, so I repeated my question and put words in his mouth, "Five?"

With a silly little smile and a slight shake of his head he mouthed, "No, fifteen."

I pulled up my towel and with a wicked little laugh said, "Hey, you better think about what you say to me. I can unplug you at any time!"

I could hear him laughing hysterically with just the expression of his face. And what do you know, he was spot on.

Early one evening while I was cuddled up to Don watching a movie, I confessed, "Don, I don't know what you're going to think, but I have a question."

I'm not sure if it was the tone of my voice or the expression on my face, but Don raised his eyebrows and looked at me with his "What now?" expression. He was generally game for any of my ideas—going to the movies, exploring museums, surprising a friend by showing up at their house, but my new idea was quite a stretch, and I needed a lot of nerve to ask. "Oh?" he mouthed.

"Well…" I was astonished how embarrassed I was to actually be asking him. "What do you think if we make love again?"

The look on his face was somewhere between surprised and beaming with pride that I wanted to be with him. "Sure," he mouthed.

"OK, I'm going to talk to the doctor about it tomorrow." I don't think Dr. Shpiner had ever dealt with a caregiver quite like me, and I knew this was going to throw him for a loop.

Our home was rather sophisticated, the first "big girl" house I had ever lived in, and for some reason, going into our library often made Doctor Shpiner say, "I always feel like I'm going to get in trouble when I come into this room; it's so adult." It was the room where all our discussions took place about Don's life—good or bad. But most of the discussions seemed to get worse, not better. We were always fighting a new set of challenges, our own war room.

"Well, Dr. Shpiner, I have a new idea, and I think I'm going to need your help. I've talked to Don, and we've decided we want to make love again. He's game and I'm game, but I think we're going to need a little help from you." Oh, the look on his face. How surprised and utterly uncomfortable he was. I think he just wanted to crawl out of my home as quickly as possible and pretend this crazy new idea had never come up.

He took his time in answering me. I'm sure he was gathering his thoughts about just how to approach this. "I had a feeling this would come up one day; I just didn't know when. I wasn't prepared for it today."

"OK, this is really embarrassing," I said, "but what the heck? My entire life is an open book now with absolutely no privacy."

"Kathi, I've got to give this some thought. There are ways to do it, but it's going to be tricky. I need to have a meeting with some of the doctors at UCLA about this."

I was astounded. He was working with us, and this was going to happen. He said he'd get back to me within a few days.

The days slipped by, and the subject didn't come up. Finally, I asked, "Dr. Shpiner, have you talked to some of the doctors to figure out what Don and I need to do about our situation? You know what I mean, right?"

"Ahh, yes, Kathi," he answered rather hesitantly. "I had a meeting with Don's team, and we've come up with a plan. It's going to be quite an undertaking. As you know, Don has a catheter, so his urologist will have to come and remove it and will stand outside the door. Don's heart Doctor will also be in the hallway to monitor for any problems that might come up. I will be in the hallway to make sure there are no pulmonary problems, and another internist will be there in case of an emergency. Along with the team, there will also be Don's nurse, respiratory therapist, and an aide."

"Fantastic. We're in."

"You are. Are you sure?"

"Absolutely," I answered. "When?"

"Ah…I needed to get your initial thoughts. To see if you really wanted to do this with all the challenges accompanying your idea." He was clearly outside his comfort zone. "I'll get back to you. I need to have another meeting with the team."

Oh my, we were full steam ahead. I couldn't wait.

A few days later, Dr. Shpiner called. He said he had met with the other doctors, and, while they were all empathetic, their final conclusion was that it would be taking too big of a chance with Don's health. There was just too much at risk, and the chance of infection could be very dangerous. I was disappointed but understood.

I shared the answer with Don. He just looked at me with his cute smile and mouthed, "Oh well. I love you for thinking about it."

I saw Dr. Shpiner for the first time a year after Don passed away at my annual physical. It truly felt like a reunion of sorts. We started reminiscing about the six and a half years we had shared. Tears came to my eyes. His too, I think. We had shared so many life-changing moments with Don, both happy and sad. I reminded him of the day I wanted one more "roll in the hay."

"You want to hear the truth, Kathi?"

"Yes," I answered with a startled question brewing inside of me. "What?"

"Kathi, there weren't any meetings with the team of doctors. I thought the bigger I made the story the less likely you would be to continue on with your idea. I should have known better. You never give up." He looked at me with the compassion of a man who understood my quest. "I felt you were setting yourself up for disappointment and decided it was best for you to always have your last good memory be from before Don's stroke, not one that was a recipe for failure and sadness."

He was a wise man, and I'm so happy he squelched my idea. In the meantime, Don felt loved, felt wanted, and he knew I was willing to go to great lengths to be with him. He also probably knew it wouldn't happen, but the energy I went through over the idea was pure bliss for him. And entertainment.

11

REWARDING REWARDS

*"I've got a great ambition to die of exhaustion
rather than boredom."*
—Thomas Carlyle

Don often said to me, "The three most important events that shaped my early life were being a Boy Scout and later an Eagle Scout, graduating from Stanford University, and flying the F-86F Sabre Jet as a fighter pilot in the US Air Force."

He was never one to accept awards, but when I received a call one day from the Boy Scouts asking if Don would consider being honored by receiving their highest honor, Distinguished Eagle Scout, I knew he'd be elated. When I asked how he felt, there was no hesitation; he mouthed a resounding, "Yes." We now had another goal to reach together, and watching his enthusiasm was thrilling. Looking forward to this night really gave us both a spring in our step—and he couldn't even walk.

Don's incredible reputation of philanthropy and service to others earned him the Distinguished Eagle Scout honor, but before anything could bear his name, he had one last goal to accomplish: Raise one million dollars for Boy Scouts of America. The amount was originally lower, but taking the easy path was never Don's way. Naively, I had no idea how much planning would need to go into this and to what extent I would be involved. All I knew was that I wanted the evening to be one of the happiest nights of Don's life. A group of Don's business associates and friends formed a committee to help raise the money for the Boy Scouts. Once the team was put together, off we went. I toured the Boy Scouts' Outdoor Education Center in Orange County, California, and was anxious to show Don photos of the various buildings, the replica of an old mine shaft where the Scouts learned about mining and geological materials, the pool, the zip line, and so many other opportunities offered to young people at the center, ending with Snake Mountain.

"I don't want my name on a building," Don mouthed, eyeing the map and photos I'd taken. "I want the mountain."

"What are you talking about?" I asked, stunned. "The mountain?"

"Yes, I want each young person to have a goal and feel accomplishment in attaining it," he said without a moment's hesitation. "I want them to say, 'I climbed Koll Mountain and reached the top.'" It was so Don to never settle for anything less than the extraordinary.

Months and months went into planning the event. The whole evening was a lovely cocktail hour and dinner, the tickets for which contributed to Don's one-million-dollar goal to get his name on a mountain. Of course, the most daunting part was raising the money, but once the invites were sent and phone calls were made, the dollars started to roll in. I'm only guessing that when people looked at the invitation, which was an exact copy of Don's actual Boy Scout card, they saw it as a way to show their love and appreciation to a man who had helped them in so many ways. The outpouring of love didn't stop with donations and tickets purchased, though. Part of planning and executing the event was finding people to donate their time, services, and expertise. It truly took a village to get the event off the ground, but with the help of some wonderful people, we were able to make it a memorable night for Don, and everyone else, too.

Former Senate Majority Leader and lung/heart transplant surgeon Bill Frist volunteered to be the keynote speaker. Don and I had been friends with Bill and his wife, Karyn, for many years, including spending time in Cabo together, even after Don's stroke. Always nice to have a doctor in the house. Jim "Watty" Watson, our charismatic longtime friend, and our friend Deborah Norville, the star of *Inside Edition,* volunteered to co-host the evening together. I called another friend, *Entertainment Tonight* host Mary Hart, to see if she would also like to be involved. With record speed she answered, "Yes, I'd love to. Anything for Don."

Deborah called me right after the Emmys and said, "I was on the Red Carpet last night interviewing stars, and Mary Hart shouted over their heads, 'I'm going to help honor Don Koll too.'" Two of TV's top television hosts, and incredibly beautiful women to boot, were like schoolgirls bubbling with excitement to honor Don.

Mary Hart, Don, and Deborah Norville

Naturally the evening would hold more excitement if Don were able to attend, but I couldn't promise that to anyone. I never knew what kind of condition Don would wake up with. He could be in great health—considering his problems, and then it all could turn on a dime. I didn't want to say he'd be there and then have the huge disappointment of him not being able to attend, but I knew how badly Don wanted to be there. He spent months dreaming about it and working towards that as his goal. It gave him another preoccupation to live for as he struggled with his challenging life. It was just one more example of how he always lived up to his motto: Exist to live, not live to exist.

Around 1:00 AM the day of the event, I gently rested my hand next to Don's face as I often did in the quietest hours. He was red hot with perspiration all over his face. I jumped out of bed, ran down the hall to the night nurse, and shouted, "Oh my God, Don's burning up. This can't be happening. Not today. Please call the doctor quickly." His temperature was 101 and climbing. We contacted the doctor, who prescribed an antibiotic, hoping it would quickly do its trick and kill whatever germ was now attacking him.

By morning, Don's fever was gone, and he spent the day mindfully preparing himself for the event. He didn't want physical therapy, visitors, or even to get out of bed. He just wanted to silently and privately rest for the evening without any distractions.

The golden hour was upon us.

"Oh, Don, I don't think I've ever seen you look more handsome," I said. He was dressed in his favorite blue suit, the one he wore when we married, and his Boy Scout tie loosely tied around his neck, somewhat hiding his trach. He mouthed, "I love you," gave me a beautiful smile and a slight thumbs-up. Years and years of therapy gave him the ability to do this, but just ever so slightly.

From the beginning, he would study his hands as I coached him. "Think, Don. You can do it. Think of being in your fighter jet, just before takeoff, giving a thumbs-up to the ground crew. Think about flying low over the desert. So low you could see the whites of the train conductor's eyes and the thumbs-up he gave you as you flew by. You would have gotten in a lot of trouble if you had been caught doing that. You can do it. Just think, think, think." And eventually, with great pride, he could do it.

Out the door we went. I drove the van with Don sitting in his wheelchair next to me, and all the medical staff sat behind us. As we rolled up to the Irvine Marriott, I felt such a sense of pride.

"Don, didn't you build this building?"

"Yes," he mouthed with a smile reserved for me. He wasn't one for bragging, but he was proud that I had remembered.

Boy Scouts standing at attention and proudly holding the American flag lined the sidewalk as I helped Don from the van. People and press crowded the background trying to get a glimpse of him, the star of the evening. I quickly rolled Don into a VIP lounge where the evening hosts, close friends, and Boy Scout officials anxiously awaited his arrival. Even Rick Cronk, the chairman of World Scout Committee and former president of the Boy Scouts of America, had flown from New York to be there for Don.

Don started to become agitated. His mood was changing. What in the heck was going on? This was getting embarrassing. Why is he getting grumpy in front of so many people excited to see him? Bill Frist was the first to say something, "Kathi, what's the matter with Don?"

"I don't know. You're a doctor. You tell me," I tensely answered.

"Take him into the room while the guests are outside having cocktails," Bill quickly suggested. "Let him see what it looks like. I think he's just anxious and doesn't know what to expect." What a brilliant idea! Why hadn't I thought of that? Months and months of planning, and Don had no idea what was behind closed doors, and he wasn't a guy who liked surprises.

Bill, Karyn, Deborah, Mary, and Watty followed us into the room. Even I wasn't prepared for what I saw, and I had planned it. A thirty-foot life-size photo of Don's Boy Scout troop backed the stage. It went from corner to corner and floor to ceiling with Don's cute little face so many years younger beaming out towards us. My friend and internationally-known event planner, Ben Bourgeois, had donated his time to help make the evening one of the greatest events Orange County had ever witnessed. The tablecloths, the flowers, the candles, the American flags. The room was sparkling and ready for nearly one thousand guests. Don was absolutely beside himself. His smile and the tears in his eyes said it all. This would be a night of joy, laughter, love, and one of the biggest gifts to Don in his lifetime.

The doors opened, and guests eagerly filed in. Many said, "It took Don Koll to get this many real estate guys together again in one room. What a reunion. What a party."

Just as we were settling down, our friend Al Checchi came up to me and said, "Kathi, I can't stay, but wanted to quickly say hi."

"What? What do you mean? You're here, and you and Kathy bought a table. Are you upset Governor Gray Davis is here?" Gray had bested Al in the 1998 California governor's race.

"No," he quickly and confidently answered. "Kathy and I were walking from the parking lot and the guard gate came down on her. She has blood all over the front of her dress, and I think her nose is broken. I'm taking her to the hospital." Off he went. Luckily, she turned out to be OK, but I missed them that evening.

A hush came over the audience as Don and I entered the room. I operated his wheelchair in very high heels, I might add. He smiled ear to ear while he nodded to friends. There was a look of respect and gentle smiles coming from the audience as we passed by, but I could also feel the sadness held deep within many hearts. Their mentor, the man they looked up to, wasn't immortal, which meant they weren't either.

It was hard to see Don Koll vulnerable. What they didn't understand was that Don was stronger than ever. He was the man they looked up to. He was still in charge. This was his bonus life. A phrase he mouthed over and over again towards the end of his life. Don Koll was teaching all of us what life was all about.

We took our spot close to the stage as the evening festivities commenced. I began to understand the respect Don had for the Boy Scouts as the crowd stood for their Presenting of the Colors as they marched by Don, the highest-ranking scout in the room. I saw youth at their best, confident and strong, as the uniformed boys led the room in reciting the Boy Scout oath:

On my honor, I will do my best. To do my duty to God and my country and to obey the Scout Law; To help other people at all times; To keep myself physically strong, mentally awake and morally straight.

Our friend Jeff Bitetti began the evening singing the "Star-Spangle Banner," followed by a catchy ballad he had composed in honor of Don, never missing a beat as he strummed his guitar. The spirited crowd were now enthusiastically swaying and clapping to the music.

Reach for the sky with all of your might
Climb the Koll Mountain and fight the good fight
Serve one another that's what life's about,
Living these values and being a Scout.

The spirit of the night was in full force and full of life. Watty read a wonderful letter from Dr. Bob Ballard, who had discovered the *Titanic* many years earlier. It seemed like just yesterday that Don and Bob had talked of searching for lost treasures. Don had financially helped with Bob's discovery of the *Bismarck* and sailed with him off the coast of Sicily, discovering a ship that had been lost at sea hundreds of years earlier. While Watty read Bob's letter, dramatic photos of the *Titanic* flashed across the screen behind him. Next were photos of Stacy Allison, the first woman to reach the summit of Mt. Everest, proudly holding the Koll flag. The theme for the evening was "From the Bottom of the Sea to the Top of the Mountain." Don was there for both—donating the seed money for Bob Ballard's Jason Foundation for Education, a project educating youth in the science and technology of the sea, and he was one of the sponsors that helped the first woman summit Everest. "The Golden Bear," Jack Nicklaus, was the next to congratulate Don via video, thanking him for their friendship and recounting the fun they had collaborating on the Palmilla and Cabo del Sol golf courses in Cabo San Lucas. They were Jack's first Signature-designed courses in Latin America.

Sen. Bill Frist, Mary Hart, Jim "Watty" Watson, Don, Kathi, Rick Cronk, Deborah Norville.

Watty and Deborah's presentation had the makings of a new act. They were amazing together, keeping the audience entertained throughout the evening with so many personal anecdotes. Mary Hart read a beautiful and very personal letter to Don from Nancy Reagan. Our friend Brad Freeman read one from President George W. Bush. Senator Frist delivered a heart-wrenching speech that went right to the core of the man Don was, and to my surprise, added some very flattering compliments about me as a loving wife and dedicated caregiver to Don.

The topper of the evening was when I rolled Don onto the stage for him to accept his award. There wasn't a dry eye in the audience, and as a surprise, Don's buddy, gold-medalist Ron Tomsic, from his college days, sang Frank Sinatra's "My Way." If you closed your eyes, you'd never know it wasn't Frank.

"Hey, Don," he teased. "This is kind of embarrassing, me singing to you. Our fraternity brothers wouldn't believe it. I'm gonna get a lot of flak for this." I could see Ron was holding back tears, but he made the evening by singing Don's favorite song. It ended the ceremony on such a sentimental and whole-hearted note.

It was nearly impossible to leave. Everyone wanted to say hi to Don, and from the smile on his face, it was obvious how much the evening had meant to him. He was existing to live and showing the world one could survive a catastrophe and still enjoy life. A life neither of us would have chosen, a life without roadmaps, but a life together on a new track, our new normal.

* * *

Everyone had been shocked by what happened to Don. His family, my family, our friends. Don had a quiet charisma. He never had to make his presence be known. You could always feel it, which was evident before his stroke, but incredibly so afterwards. He was bigger than life, and no one wanted to see their superhero like that. Men seemed to be especially vulnerable to his plight, having difficulties coming to grips with the situation. "If it could happen to Don Koll, it could happen to me," they said. "I can't visit Don Koll and see him different from the man I know." They didn't understand that Don was now a man far beyond the man they knew. He embarked on a life that left all of his other achievements in the dust. He tested his true spirit, and in the end, he passed with flying colors. Proud doesn't come close to explaining my feelings for the path he chose and how he chose to conquer it.

At the time of Don's stroke there was a real estate convention going on in Los Angeles called the International Council of Shopping Centers: ICSC. I heard that Mike Matkins, a partner at Allen Matkins law firm, got up in front of two thousand people in the audience and made the announcement that Don Koll had suffered a severe stroke and probably wouldn't live long. Apparently, a stunned silence fell upon the room.

Six weeks before Don died, I stood in front of over nine hundred people, Don by my side, at the California Club in Los Angeles, where Don was being honored as the first Stanford Professional in Real Estate recipient, an honor bestowed by the esteemed Stanford alumni group SPIRE. With Don sitting in his wheelchair on stage beside me, *The Diving Bell and the Butterfly* again crossed my mind. I thought about the similarities and what the audience would be thinking. Deep down, I felt it was my last chance to speak for him in front of a large crowd and say the things for Don I knew he would want everyone to hear.

"Many of you were in the audience at the ICSC six and a half years ago when an announcement was made that Don Koll had suffered a stroke and probably wouldn't make it." Then as now, the audience was stunned. I paused, proudly gazing at Don, then looked intently at the audience and continued, "But Don knew better."

The crowd broke into a thunderous applause, and Don grinned from ear to ear, acknowledging the feelings that were being showered upon him that evening. As he looked out over his peers, he mouthed, "I'm still here." Looking at the hundreds of people in front of me, I thought of some important things they should know about my husband that they probably hadn't thought of. Things he might want me to share.

"Recently, I finally got the guts to ask Don some questions," I said, "and I want to share them with you. I asked him, 'Don, if you had your life to do all over again, would you do anything differently?'"

Before I could give the audience the answer he had shared with me, he mouthed, "NO."

"So, I asked him, 'Don, are you adjusted to your life?'"

Quickly he mouthed, "YES."

"Don, are you happy?"

Without a second of hesitation he gave his most beautiful Don Koll grin and mouthed, "ABSOLUTELY."

The standing ovation he received was the culmination of his life's achievements. The most important of which was that, beyond all odds, he was there that evening. Everyone had tears running down their faces, applauding in admiration of a man who truly lived his life in good times and in bad, with ups and downs and without a word of complaining. "You can't worry about things you can't change," he always said to me. In the toughest time of his life he lived the words he always advised others to live by with grace and dignity. Seeing him realize the love in the room that was pouring out to him was one of the happiest moments in my life.

12

SWEET SORROW

*"Parting is such sweet sorrow that I shall say
goodnight till it be morrow."*
—William Shakespeare

Eighteen trips later, a number of near-death experiences, and many extraordinarily happy memories behind us, we were sitting on our Cabo veranda, waiting for the ambulance to arrive to take us to the airport and back home to California, with the knowledge we'd be back within a couple of months.

Our trips to Cabo were not devoid of drama, and along with one crisis after another, I always held a lingering fear in the back of my mind that being there alone with Don would be depressing for both of us. I'm not sure why I came to this conclusion, but because of my insecurity, I made sure we were always surrounded by friends and family to distract us. I think the reality was that I knew every day of Don's life was a precious gift. The thought of something happening to him so far away, out of the US, without close family or friends with me was frightening.

The struggle I was experiencing with Don was compounded by the constant guilt I felt not spending enough time with my brother Don. He, who had for the most part raised me and will always be one of the most influential people of my life, was biding his time patiently on the side. I knew through friends he constantly worried about the stress I was going through. He'd had a lifetime of his own problems, though. When I was a child, he survived a brutal beating from a burglar that left him in the hospital unconscious for a month. After his release, my parents had him share my room for a few weeks so he wouldn't be alone. Years later, I nursed him back to health after open-heart surgery and then again after a serious nine-hour Whipple operation. His constant struggle, though, was neuropathy as a result of diabetes. During the six and a half years my husband was ill, he graciously stepped aside and rarely mentioned his health problems, but I knew he was experiencing great pain from the neuropathy.

I couldn't shake the feeling I had abandoned him. I just couldn't give him the energy and closeness I always had, because my life was consumed with keeping my head above water with my husband, Don. Thanksgiving was a few weeks away, and Don and I had planned to go to Mexico. This was our first visit to be by ourselves, other than the professional care personnel, for a couple of weeks. The family was arriving just before the holiday. I didn't invite my brother because the house was full, and I knew the commotion with energetic babies would frustrate him—a decision I will forever regret making.

After Don and I arrived and took the normal five days for him to regain his strength from traveling, we fell into a new Cabo routine. To my surprise, I loved being there alone with him.

By then, Don was on dialysis, a choice he made when it was discovered his kidneys were failing. He simply wouldn't give up, and as complicated and uncomfortable as it was, he wanted to do it. He was hooked into the machine for five hours early in the morning as he slept. I would get up and head off to play golf by myself. Friends would see me and ask me to join them, but I wanted this time to be alone, uninterrupted, to gather my thoughts. By the time I returned home, Don would be finished with his treatment, bathed and raring to go to the pool where we would stay for the rest of the day into the night. Don reclined in his swim trunks with tubes and medications hanging from IV poles. Me, reading next to him. I know I'm not painting an ideal

Don and Kathi in Cabo

picture, but it was. The two weeks we were there alone were the best time I had with Don during those eighteen trips. There was a wonderful peacefulness and contentment I wasn't expecting. Normally Don would be in bed by 8:00 PM, but on that trip, he resisted. We spent evenings on the veranda listening to music, me reading to him. Then we'd dance our custom dance of me gliding him across the floor in his wheelchair as our favorite music played, the moon dancing across the water. Thoughts of my daughter Brooke and son-in-law Chris' wedding floated through my mind. Don had played a trick on Chris and me by saying "no" when Chris first asked for Brooke's hand in marriage. The poor man was frozen, and I was shocked. When he said yes, we broke out the Dom Perignon to celebrate. Even Don drank some from a spoon as we sipped from our crystal flutes. We were excited and honored that they chose to have their wedding at our home in Cabo. There wasn't a dry eye in the house as I spun him in his wheelchair while our song, "Unforgettable," played. He never took his eyes off of me and mouthed every word of the song.

Dancing on the veranda

"Don, what do you think we do this again in February?"

"Yes," he quickly mouthed. Our new normal was at its best.

I called my brother and said, "How about you fly down here and spend a week with us before all the family commotion starts?" He was never one for change or flexibility, and the thought of quickly jumping on a plane was a stretch, but I convinced him. I could always convince my big brother; I had him wrapped around my little finger. At the same time, a friend and her daughter-in-law asked if they could spend a few days with me. I didn't tell my brother until he arrived that a bit of his time was going to compete with two other guests. He wasn't happy about it at first, but when they arrived, he fell head-over-heels for the daughter-in-law. I don't mean in a romantic way, but he just adored everything about her. It was sweet to watch, and she was a good sport paying a lot of attention to him. The night before he left, he hosted all of us for dinner at the One and Only Palmilla. Don sold the hotel years earlier, and to his dismay, the words 'One and Only' were clunkily attached. I hadn't seen my brother having so much fun in a long time. There was lots of laughter, and the conversation was flowing from one topic to another. The next morning as he was leaving the house, he wrapped his arms around me and said, "This was one of the best vacations I've ever had."

I assumed he was going to have Thanksgiving with friends, but learned later he didn't. Rogelio, who had worked for me and Don for years, picked him up from the airport. A year later, Rogelio told me that when my brother Don got in the car, he went on and on about how fun the week was but turned serious when he said, "I'm worried about my sister. Living with her for the week opened my eyes to how truly difficult her life is. What will happen if I die before Don? Who will take care of my sister?"

I understood exactly how he felt. My biggest fear was what would happen to my husband, Don, if I died first. Who would take care of him? Rogelio tried to put my brother's mind at peace, reminding him I had loving and involved children who would always look after me. He wasn't convinced. He was worried he wouldn't be there. "I'll take care of Mame," Rogelio assured him.

Why is the last day of a vacation always the most beautiful? The day that makes you feel like you haven't done nearly what you've wanted to do and every last idea needs to be squeezed in as if it'll never happen again.

I awoke earlier than usual. The lace curtains were drawn, but through them I could make out the silhouette of palm trees swaying in the cool Baja breeze. The sun was just coming up. Don's dialysis had already started, and as I opened my eyes, he was staring at me. I wondered how long he had been looking at me and what thoughts were going through his mind. Once he knew I was awake, he simply smiled and mouthed, "I love you." I pulled myself closer to him and slowly kissed his lips. Over his shoulder I could see the sun floating on the horizon with moored fishing boats bobbing in the water. How could a day start out any better? The silent minutes of the morning were always my favorite, and the knowledge of other people in the room had long ceased to bother me. I knew how to blank them out of my mind and give us stolen little moments that were our treasured little secret.

Leaving the house in Mexico was always bittersweet. There wasn't time for therapy or lounging by the pool, but there was time to sit together on the veranda until the transport ambulance arrived. My daughter Jennifer her husband, Rick, and their children were still at the house. Together we lingered after breakfast. Don seemed to savor every last moment.

I could barely hear the telephone ringing in the background, competing with the waves crashing on the rocks below. Yolanda, who has worked for me for many years, came out of the kitchen and said, "Señora Koll, your son, Kevin, is on the phone."

"Hi, Kevin, how was your flight home?" I asked.

"Everything was fine. When are you coming back?" he questioned with an urgency in his voice.

"The ambulance is outside, and we're just about to get Don on the stretcher and drive to the airport," I answered.

"How long do you think it will take you?" he asked.

"I guess door-to-door we'll be back within four or five hours, why?"

"I was just wondering," he said, but I sensed something wrong in his voice. It just wasn't a normal conversation and quickly became apparent he was trying to keep something from me.

"Kevin, is everything OK?"

"Aww, Mom, Uncle Don tripped and has gotten hurt," he answered with a noticeable quiver in his voice.

"Not again. I keep telling him he needs to use the cane you gave him. The neuropathy in his feet is causing him a lot of trouble, and he's going to break a hip or something. Put him on the phone."

"He can't come to the phone, Mom."

"What do you mean he can't come to the phone? Put him on the phone. I need to talk to him."

"The paramedics are here checking him out, so he can't talk to you."

"What?" I was getting an uneasy feeling in my stomach. "Well, put the phone up to his ear."

"Mom, he's in the ambulance on the way to the hospital. Please hurry home, Mom. I think you need to hurry."

Kevin caught me off guard. It couldn't be that serious. It just had to be my brother's urgency for me to get back. He never let the doctors do anything on him without my OK. Once, he was in recovery after a surgery, and the morphine was causing problems. He wouldn't do anything for the medical staff until I arrived. He was insistent that I sign off on everything while he wasn't in peak condition.

I didn't know what to think or which way to turn. Jennifer and Rick had been intently listening to my conversation. By the time I got off the phone, Jennifer was crying. "Mom, has something happened to Uncle Don?"

"Something's always happening to him. I'm sure it's nothing," I said, "but Kevin says we should hurry."

I didn't want to think anything had happened, and sounding confident made me feel like it hadn't. Jennifer and her family were about to leave for their flight home, and I figured we'd land in LA near the same time to go to the hospital and see what was going on.

Don had also witnessed my conversation. "What's going on with your brother?" he mouthed.

"I'm not sure, Don. All I know is I need to get home."

I called Dr. Shpiner at UCLA and asked if he could call the emergency hospital in Orange County my brother had been taken to. The ride to the airport in the ambulance was much different this time. Normally, I sat next to Don, reliving the fun weeks we had just enjoyed, trying to get his mind off his uncomfortable and bumpy drive. This time there was a silence and uncomfortable thickness in the air. The ride seemed like it was taking forever. Thoughts were going through my mind that had no business being there. Thoughts I didn't want and thoughts I never believed would really come true. Dark thoughts that couldn't be true. Nothing bad could happen to my brother. I felt so helpless. The other part of my soul was struggling, and I wasn't with him. I had to get home; he needed me. I knew he was scared without me being there to let him know all was OK.

We got to the airport and through security in record time. Just as the door to the plane was closing, my phone rang. An aching feeling pulled at my stomach, a feeling so painful I didn't want to answer the phone. "Hello?"

"Kathi," Dr. Shpiner's voice rang in my ear, "I talked to the doctor at the hospital. For all practical purposes, your brother is gone. He's still alive, but won't be for long. I'm so sorry."

"No, no, no," I cried. This couldn't be happening. "No, God, please don't take him from me. Please don't take him from me." It was apparent to everyone within eyesight of me that what I had heard wasn't good. I didn't want to share this with Don. He was too fragile to hear such devastating news. I didn't know how it would affect him. At the same time, I was falling apart in silence. I couldn't let him see what was happening to me, but the reality was that it felt like I was trying to hang on to space by the tips of my fingers. A space that wasn't there. There was nothing.

The DK medical team sat motionlessly looking down at the floor, and I felt so alone. Every once in a while I caught the eyes of one of them glancing towards me, and they passed a slight, comforting smile my way. No one talked. There was nothing to talk about. I couldn't ask Don for strength as I sat next to him in his fragile condition. I couldn't call my brother for help. I didn't know where to turn, other than to look straight ahead and think, try to make sense and reason out of what I was living. There was no sense. There was no sensibility. Why was God taking the other most important person in my life away from me?

The flight home was the longest flight I've ever experienced. The normal two hours felt like a detour through Purgatory. When we finally landed, my cell phone started ringing. It was Kevin. "Mom, hurry. Mom, you have to hurry."

I drove down the freeway as fast as I could. It was the same freeway I had driven my entire life, the same freeway I had driven in the same state of mind six and a half years earlier trying to get to my husband. Time had become a time bomb. Kevin stayed on the phone, giving me updates and directions. Softly and with a true sense of sorrow in his voice, he repeatedly said, "Are you almost here, Mom? You need to hurry, Mom."

I was confused about why my brother had not been taken to Hoag, the hospital near our home, until I found out it wasn't a critical care hospital, so he was taken to the one that was. I had never been there, and I was overcome with frustration having to find my way to a completely foreign place. I was tearing through unknown streets, scared I wouldn't get there in time. But in time for what? My mind was racing with all sorts of thoughts, mostly that what was happening wasn't really happening. I needed more time. He couldn't leave without a proper goodbye.

When I reached the hospital, Kevin and his wife, Melissa, were waiting for me on the front steps. They were visibly shaken, and the severity of what I was about to see was written all over their faces.

We hugged tightly for a brief moment before they led me into the hospital, down the corridor, and through the tightly secured ICU doors. As we walked into my brother's room, Kevin softly said, "Uncle Don, my mom is here. I told you she would get here." The lights were dim, and other than the melodic hum of the respirator, there was a deafening silence. My brother was on life support.

I laid my head on his chest as tears welled up in my eyes. I loved him so much. My entire life with him passed in front of me in slow motion. I felt his hand walking me into my new school. I saw him swimming towards me in the pool. I saw the smile on his face when I got my first car. I saw him at the hospital for the birth of my first baby. I saw everything in a matter of moments. I raised my head and squeezed his hand as I whispered in his ear how much I loved him and thanked him for the life he had given me. His breathing changed. He was trying to say something. He knew he was loved.

Monsignor Baird from my church in Newport Beach arrived. Surrounded by my three children, Jennifer, Kevin, and Brook, and my daughter-in-law, Melissa, whom Uncle Don adored, he was given his last rites. I know it was just as he would have wanted it. Prayers for the repose of his soul and the closest, most important people in his life with him. Within minutes he was gone.

When I look back, I think about how much I would have changed. I would have given my brother a consistent slot of time every week, written in ink on the calendar. The intention was there, but time slipped away so quickly with all that was going on with my husband, Don. I did talk to my brother almost every day and see him most weeks, but I've learned that consistency for someone ill or lonely is much better. That standing date is always there.

13

THE NEXT ROOM

"I have only slipped away into the next room.
Nothing has happened. Everything remains exactly as it was.
I am I, and you are you, and the old life that we lived
so fondly together is untouched, unchanged."
—Henry Scott-Holland

The five of us walked out of the room. It was so hard to leave him there all alone. He couldn't be gone. He was just sleeping. No, he was gone, and the deep sorrow we all felt was indescribable. We huddled together in a circle in the hallway with our arms tightly wrapped around each other. The tighter we hugged the harder we cried. I don't think I ever felt closer to my children.

None of us could bear the thought of leaving him in this strange place. I don't think we believed the reality of what was happening and were waiting for something miraculous to take over. We couldn't lose him like this. We needed more time to tie up all the loose ends. We had so many questions for him, now forever unanswered. We wanted to spend more days just focused on him. He needed us; we needed him. My brother, their Uncle Don, the strength of our little family. We walked down the long corridor and out into the cold wet air, shivering. I'm not sure if it was from the weather or from the unfathomable sadness chilling us to the bone.

Jennifer and Brooke said they'd come home and stay with me to help with the next steps. A funeral was what they meant. My next step was breaking the news to Don.

I wasn't sure how this would affect Don emotionally. I walked into our home around 1:00 AM, took a deep breath, and headed straight down the hallway towards our bedroom. All the lights were on, but the house was very quiet. Everyone there had been waiting for my news, hoping it wasn't what they feared. I peeked into our bedroom and saw Don still awake, looking up at the ceiling.

"Why isn't Don asleep yet, and why is he still in the clothes he wore coming home from Mexico?" I asked the nurse.

"He refused to change. He doesn't want anyone near him," she answered tearfully. "He's been waiting for you, Kathi."

I slowly walked into our room, dreading the difficult task ahead of me.

I lay down next to Don, put my arms around him and whispered what happened into his ear. I held him tightly, as tight as I ever had, and quietly cried myself to sleep.

Within a few short hours, the morning light filled our room with sunshine and warmth. I was still clinging to Don and thinking about how the room had always been so cheerful with its soft yellow walls and view through the trees towards the mountains and the Pacific beyond. I closed my eyes and thought about the first morning Don and I had lived in the house.

"You'll never sit in the garden," I could hear Don saying. "You'll think it's too cold out there with the westerly wind blowing off the ocean."

"Don, there's a mountain range in between. I don't think we'll feel the cool westerly." We never did and spent years in that beautiful garden from sunup to sundown. I didn't see the beauty of anything this day. I was numb from a reality I once again found myself having to face. A reality that was creeping in and filling my heart with a pain that felt like a thousand needles piercing its core. It was a new day to live, a new day to challenge never-ending obstacles with newfound successes, but I didn't have the courage to face the day this time. Don was once again staring at me. I watched him through my barely open eyes, hoping he'd think I was still asleep. I couldn't let him see me falling apart.

I sprang out of bed and quickly ran into my small bathroom. My only refuge. I sat on the floor, head buried in my hands, and wept. "God, why do you keep doing these things to me?" Once again, I found myself in a sea of sorrow.

I pulled myself together and tiptoed past Don without him seeing me. I found my girls in the kitchen, eyes red and swollen. Neither had slept.

The three of us sat around the kitchen table in disbelief. I don't know what I would have done without them. Their presence was the force that helped me start the torturous exercise of planning the funeral.

I knew the one spot my brother would love to have his funeral would be at his alma mater, Loyola High School. I made a few calls, and within a couple of hours, we were in the rectory planning the last celebration of Uncle Don's life. The school didn't look like one would expect in California. It could have easily been in the middle of Connecticut.

By the time I got home, I was exhausted. The adrenalin I had been running on was completely out of fuel. Even collapsing onto my bed was too much energy.

I could feel Don's eyes watching me. The moment he caught my glance, he mouthed, "What happened to your brother?"

"What happened to my brother?" I asked, beside myself. "Don, did you not hear what I told you last night?"

Don looked at me, his still-sharp mind searching for what could elicit this reaction from me. Confusion, concern, love, and the pain that he couldn't hug me permeated the air between us.

"Oh, no...Don. My brother died last night."

I sat on the edge of the bed, my eyes glancing down towards the coverlet, not knowing what to do. I looked at every thread of that coverlet for what must have been forever. I tried to hold in my tears, but it was impossible. I looked up at Don, and he was crying. My husband, who couldn't utter a sound, was sobbing. He looked so helpless. I put my arms around him the best I could, our tearstained faces pressed together. I knew he wanted to hold me, and I so needed him to, but he couldn't raise his arms. God, he couldn't raise his arms.

I was freefalling in a Grand Canyon of sadness I could no longer disguise. I could barely stop crying. Every time I walked into our room Don was staring at me. He never took his eyes off of me, and each time our eyes met he simply mouthed, "I love you."

My brother had been gone since Tuesday evening, but Don heard the news Wednesday afternoon. It was Thursday, and Don refused to get dressed in the morning. He didn't want any medical staff near him, wouldn't do any of his therapies—physical, speech, nothing. He didn't care about the TV. All he did was watch me and mouth, "I love you."

I felt something was very different, and there was a definite change in Don's appearance. I kept wondering what it was. Was "I love you" his way of taking care of me? Was it his way of letting me know he was there for me? He seemed so at peace and at the same time seemed to be deep in thought. There was an aura about him that I couldn't put my finger on. It was a look I had never seen on Don, before or after his stroke.

I glanced towards him, put my hand on his cheek, and told him how much I loved him and how much he meant to me. Once again, he didn't say anything other than, "I love you." I don't think he had anything else to say. The look in his eyes, his skin, his demeanor, it was all different. Something was going on. He looked like an angel.

Friday morning, Don's main line was having problems, which meant we needed to go to the hospital. It wasn't an emergency but needed attention. We loaded Don into the van and off we went. Don always insisted I be the one to drive. The van was huge and quite a beast to maneuver. The lift for the wheelchair alone was 1,200 pounds. At first it felt like it took two blocks to stop, but by now, I could drive it like a Porsche. I'd often mimic Don and say, "I have the need for speed," while the medical personnel braced themselves in the back. Don loved our adventures. Our drives to the Santa Monica beach, by the home he grew up in at Hancock Park, by office buildings he had built or had wanted to build, by new projects popping up all around town. Don securely strapped into his wheelchair next to me on the passenger side. These were our escape moments.

After so many years, we were quasi-celebrities at the UCLA emergency ward. Early on, Dr. Shpiner came up with the brilliant idea of having all Don's procedures done there. The doctors could easily come to him versus him going to them. This day, I was so exhausted that the staff brought in another gurney and placed it next to Don for me to sleep on. I just couldn't move.

Soon after Don's procedure, he became very impatient and kept mouthing, "Let's go, let's go." It was a scramble to get out of there quick enough to satisfy him. In rushing, we left some wheelchair parts behind.

"Don, you're making me so uptight I've forgotten some of your things. Now we have to go back." He merely rolled his eyes impatiently.

It was good to get home again and feel the security of our room, our safe place, but what was going on with Don? I spent the rest of the day next to him napping and trying to get my arms around the enormity of it all. My girls were going through photos of my brother in the other room, picking songs for the service and working on the minute details of planning my brother's funeral. As I peeked in on them, we'd cry through our sadness and laugh as we recalled typical Uncle Don stories. I chose December 7th for the service, my birthday. I couldn't think of a better tribute to my brother than to forever share that day with him.

Brooke was nine months pregnant. I was worried about the stress all this drama was putting on her pregnancy. I walked into the library where the girls were still working and said, "Let's run down the hill and get a quick dinner. Don's getting ready for bed, which will take about an hour. I don't want him to know I've left; he thinks I'm helping you. Let's go."

Life hadn't changed at my favorite little French bistro on Sunset Boulevard. The escape was a welcome break for us. The world was going on, even though ours seemed to have come to a screeching halt.

My phone started ringing just as we were leaving.

"Kathi, come home. Come home fast. Don's not breathing," Don's nurse said with a panicked voice.

"What do you mean he's not breathing?" I yelled. "He's on a respirator. How could he not be breathing? That's impossible."

"I don't know. Just hurry. The paramedics are here."

I was shaking uncontrollably as I raced up the hill toward my house. Jennifer wanted to drive, but she was in no better condition than I was. "No, God, please don't take him from me." I cried uncontrollably as I turned the curve towards the house. "God, please, please, please, don't do this to me."

The gravity of the situation hit me at the sight of our street closed off by three fire engines and seven police cars. I slammed on the brakes, leaped out of the car, and ran by the blockade, yelling, "This is my house." Every light inside was on. I ran down the hallway to our bedroom. It was filled with police officers, firemen, and paramedics heroically working on Don. I knelt down next to him and yelled into his ear, "Don, don't give up. Don, you can do it. Don't leave me. You can make it; you can make it. Don, don't leave me. Please, Don, don't leave me."

Brooke and Jennifer stood off to the side sobbing as a few policemen tried to comfort them. All of a sudden, Brooke got up on the bed next to Don, her large belly in front of her, and said, "Step-Daddy-O, you've got to meet my baby." With that Don got color in his face. He heard her. He wanted to live.

The paramedics felt Don was stabilized enough to get him to the hospital. Dr. Shpiner arrived and jumped into the back of the ambulance with Don. I sat in the front as we sped off towards the hospital. Don was surrounded by the paramedics and Dr. Shpiner, all administering lifesaving measures on him. Measures I had never witnessed being done on him before. I was in shock. My prayers, my hope, and their expertise had to work. They just had to work. I couldn't lose Don today.

Our welcome at UCLA was different than I had ever witnessed before. We'd had close calls, but all paled in comparison to this. The team was ready for him, and he was quickly swept into an emergency operating room, me at his side. By then, my knowledge of Don's situation had given me the vocabulary and stamina for anything that came our way. No one questioned why the wife was in the room. I found out later the doctors thought I was Don's head nurse.

Dr. Shpiner took me aside and said, "Kathi, it's serious, but he's surprised us before, I think he might just make it." Hopeful optimism couldn't hurt.

Miraculously, Don had not suffered a stroke, and his brain didn't show any more damage than the first stroke six years earlier, but he wasn't regaining consciousness. The doctors decided to put him into a hypothermic coma to slow down any possible further damage, study what was happening to him, and give his body a chance to slowly heal as he was brought back. Time stood still during those eighteen hours. I hoped he'd come back and give me that angelic, "I love you." Realistically, though, I was scared.

As Don was slowly brought back out of his coma, the prognosis didn't look good. He wasn't responding. Dr. Shpiner told me to try and get some rest. Nothing was going to happen right away, but I couldn't bear to leave Don alone. Four of the girls who had worked with him from the beginning volunteered to stay by his side through the night. They gave him a sort of wake. I know he must have loved it. They danced, they sang and they whispered all their deep, dark secrets into his ear.

Early the next morning, Dr. Shpiner called and said, "Kathi, I've been at UCLA for a long time, and I've never witnessed anything like what's going on right now. There is a long line outside the ICU doors all the way to Don's bedside of many of the medical personnel who have ever worked for Don." The word had spread quickly that he was failing, and people had driven from all over Southern California to say goodbye. They were dressed in isolation garb, and one by one, they were paying their respects.

As I did the week before, I telephoned Monsignor Baird and asked if he could administer the last rites. I called our family and close friends. Everyone was given their time to say goodbye. The only request I had was to be alone with him at the end.

It was December 6th. The night before my birthday. The evening before my brother's funeral. The lights were dim, and our song "Unforgettable" was softly playing in the background. I held Don in my arms for the first time in many years without tubes and wires. Slowly and silently, the love of my life slipped away from me.

* * *

Years earlier the doctors had told me Don would go when he was ready. I didn't understand what they meant at the time. Yes—Don did it his way. He used the days after my brother's death to think. His *I love you*s were also his goodbyes.

On December 7, 2011, as I walked down the aisle of Loyola High School's chapel, I couldn't help but think of my two Dons as one. Two people, but one force in my life. My family and I took our places in the front row, and as the priest finished his opening homily, he looked at the congregation and asked for prayers for my brother Don Robinson and also for the soul of Don Koll, who had passed away the evening before. There was a noticeable gasp and unquestionable shock, followed by the sound of many people crying. No one could believe what they had just heard. My two Dons were gone, but now I had two angels to forever look down upon me.

The loves of my life were gone, and life as I knew it would never be the same.

14

IS THERE A HOW-TO BOOK?

"Life is either a daring adventure or nothing at all."
—Helen Keller

Living with a multitude of people took a long time to get used to—I'm not actually sure if I ever did—but it was a bittersweet experience, because I was at quite a loss once they were gone. They had truly become family to me. Sort of the sorority I never belonged to. They listened to my problems, watched me cry, followed the lives of my family. They were there for the birth of each grandchild. They helped me pick what to wear when I was invited to dinner with friends. They helped me pack when I had a little weekend getaway. Their absence was as surrounding as their presence. I still miss them.

Forging a new life is difficult and takes so much work, but remember the famous quote from Churchill: "Never, never, never, never give up." Well, that couldn't apply more. Life is what we make it, and it comes with a price that we pay in tenacity.

The first year after the death of my brother and husband are almost a blank now. Most of my time was spent with family and a few close friends. If I wasn't working, I was sitting on the beach playing with my grandchildren. Just going to a luncheon was difficult. It still is, but because they're boring. I cried a lot—and when I say a lot, I mean *a lot*. One day, I was sitting in my bedroom sobbing, and I thought, *Who am I crying about?* I wasn't thinking about one Don in particular. I was just crying. It was bizarre to be so sad, to be in so much pain and not know who it was for at any given moment.

I said to myself, "OK, now I'm going to focus on my husband and cry over him. Now it's my brother's turn." I know it sounds weird, but I had to work at separating the two. Otherwise, my mind was an endless mess of confusion. It allowed me the chance to properly mourn each one in order to find the strength to move forward.

My two losses were completely different. The sudden and unexpected death of my brother was the most challenging. I have no regrets of the life with my husband, but so many loose ends with my brother that will now be impossible to tie. I've learned to move on without as much pain, but there will always be a loss deep within.

Being a widow has been very difficult, to say the least. Going back into that little cage of comfort is tempting, but will never bring me happiness to move on with a new chapter in my life. I hope I never look at life as only yesterday and today. I want to continue to have new adventures and stories that will also become yesterday.

Friends will say, "Kathi, you need to learn how to be alone. I have quiet dinners with my husband all the time and just watch TV." As much as I love them for caring about my well-being, and I know they're coming from a helpful place, the operative word is "husband" or whomever they're with. He might be working in the garage or reading the paper in another room, but he's still there. I had never lived alone. I went from my parents' home to being married at eighteen. I raised three children, and my youngest was still home when I married Don. When he became sick, I had a multitude of people coming and going. The day he died was the first time I found myself completely alone.

Being in the midst of this self-reinvention is one of my biggest challenges yet. It's a new chapter that I'm working on and little by little finding success. I'm pushing myself out of my comfort zone, and each time has brought new strength and—pleasure too. As difficult as it is, I'm moving forward with my life, because it's important to understand—not only for others but also for myself—that *my* life hasn't stopped. I can't deny that bittersweet thoughts often go through my mind, but I'm making the familiar also new. I'm trying to make new memories apart from the ones with Don. He will always be there, way down in a corner of my heart, but not moving forward is losing the wonderful opportunity at a new life. I had an almost perfect life disrupted by death, which is unquestionably the worst feeling in the world. It's not something that was chosen, but something that I was stuck with.

The November after Don's death, not even a full year later, I received a brochure in the mail from Stanford Travel. Since Don had graduated from there, I was on their mailing list. I peered through the pages, thinking of all the wonderful places I had been to with Don, imagining never getting to go to again. My family was all together for Thanksgiving, and we started talking about it. The hiking trip in the Pyrenees looked intriguing. Something I had never done or thought about doing.

"Kathi, this looks fantastic," said my son-in-law Rick. "You should do it."

"Are you kidding?" I answered. "I can't go alone. I won't know a soul. I've never gone anywhere alone in my entire life. I'll be lonely; I'll get sad."

"If you're lonely and sad, get on a plane and come home." Rick made sense.

I started seriously thinking about it till one morning I awakened and said to myself, *Screw it. What do I have to lose other than a missed opportunity?* Don used to always say, "Kathi, it's the things in life you don't do that you most regret." The Spain trip was suddenly a reality.

In my nervous anticipation, I mentioned the trip to some new friends I was having dinner with. "We're from Sweden and live there half the year. How about visiting us first?" they suggested. Before I knew it I was on my way, with my first stop at a beautiful home situated on an island in the archipelago. They welcomed me with open arms *and* Swedish meatballs.

I arrived in June, when the sun barely sets. They included me at their Summer Solstice party, and after each traditional song was a downing of schnapps. To my surprise there was an additional song; they played "Star-Spangled Banner" in my honor, and of course, it was followed by more schnapps. I hated leaving the warmth of this family, but the day came, and I was off to my hiking adventure.

I was a nervous wreck as the plane started to descend over the town of Pamplona. *What in the heck am I doing?* I thought. The familiar question formed a pit in my stomach as I peered through the window at the beautiful countryside, rolling hills, and red-tiled roofs. *Will I find my way? Will the group be nice? Will I be an oddball alone?* Everything was going through my mind. As I left the baggage area, I spotted a man with a Stanford sign. So far, so good.

"Are you Kathi?" he questioned. "You're early and the first. Another couple is also arriving early, so you're going to take a van with them to our first spot, St. Jean-Pied-de-Port. The rest of the group will arrive later."

The group was amazing. There were twenty of us, mostly couples plus a few singles like me. From the get-go, I felt embraced. I had absolutely no idea what the hike would be like. I had fantasized about winding trails along streams, small quaint villages, and gentle sloping hills. Oh my, yes, that was all there, but most of the time was a grueling hike in the mountains. Twelve to fifteen miles per day. I didn't dare let on how strenuous it was for me and was secretly proud of myself that I was keeping up.

I quickly learned that being in the front to middle of the pack was the secret. It meant longer rest time as we waited for the slower ones. Part of our group was Dr. Roberto D'Alimonte, professor of political science and a journalist engaged by Stanford to lecture on the politics and current events in Spain. Our guides, Peter Watson and Ben Littlewood, had incredible knowledge not only of the terrain, but also of the political and historical complexity of the region. For a girl who never much cared for school, I was soaking up as much knowledge as possible. I was also soaking in the tub each morning. I was so sore it was the only way I could get my tired bones moving.

It was all so fascinating and exhilarating, just the cup of tea I needed to get me going on my new life moving forward. Learning new things and meeting entirely new people, some of whom I have become very close friends with. The group varied from journalists to families to doctors. I asked the psychiatrist of the group if he had ever hypnotized anyone, and with his affirmative answer, asked if he'd hypnotize me.

"Why do you want to be hypnotized?" he asked with a puzzled look on his face.

"If the hypnosis works, I could walk faster, not tire too easily, remember each blade of grass."

What can I say? It worked. It's still the day I remember more clearly than any of the others. I also realized for the first time since Don's death that there are other men in the world who might also intrigue me as a friend or future partner. I was new to being alone, and the little bit of dating I'd done had been challenging—each person had an agenda that left me wondering what I was really supposed to do.

I met a wonderful man during my hike. His quiet charisma, school-boy shyness, and impressive intellect reminded me of Don— just a genuinely good person with no ulterior plans. His demeanor, compassion, and respect for his family led me to see there can be a life going forward with a quality person. It had been only two years since my Dons passed, and this man was like an angel sent from both of them. He had no agenda other than companionship on the trail. He shared lovely stories about his life and family, and gave ear to the challenges of my past with Don and life going forward. He listened compassionately to my memories of my husband and my brother and felt it was good they hold a part of my heart. His counsel came at just the right time, and I so deeply appreciate his kindness.

I believe that, as I move forward, the next person in my life has to be someone who can embrace and accept my past. My parents, brothers, and husband will always have a part of my heart. The next person will also have that. I have a giant section waiting, and he will fill the sections open to a new life and be ever so equal to all the people in my life who have gotten me to where I am today. I look forward to this next person showing me new horizons, eager to share in my thirst to learn and see a life I haven't experienced.

Trying to step into a new life also opened up the question: What to do about my ring? Do I wear it? Am I supposed to take it off?

I noticed after Don died people would glance at my hand. It was a very uncomfortable feeling. I knew what they were thinking, and I didn't know what I was supposed to do. I felt uncomfortable knowing they were thinking about it, and I was thinking about it, but no one was mentioning it. This inevitably leads to things said from a place of love, but that often end up feeling hurtful in the moment. One of my friends said, "When you feel ready to take off your ring, that doesn't mean you can't wear it around your neck." He was right, but it was a leap that's easier said than done. I hadn't thought about it before nor read what the proper thing to do was or if there even was a proper thing to do.

I came to my own conclusion. If I was to move forward and date, I needed to take off my ring. There's no right or wrong answer, but it was the conclusion I came to for myself. Not only was it hard, from a feeling of security, but I had worn a wedding ring every year but one since I was eighteen. It was part of my existence. An eleventh finger.

One afternoon, I met my daughter Brooke at the beach. We took a bottle of wine, toasted Don, and I took off my ring. I thought the timing was right, but as it turned out, it wasn't. I couldn't stand looking at my bare finger. I felt naked. I felt empty. I felt like a loser. I felt so alone. Within two days I put it right back on. Over the next few weeks I started taking it off and on for practice until I finally started to get comfortable with it off.

Sitting in the library of my home in Mexico, the last spot I shared happiness with my two Dons, I looked at the pictures surrounding me on the shelves and thought about how to move on. Which photos to take off the shelf. Which new ones to make room for. I refuse to be frozen in time. My life is going to go on, and I'm determined it's going to be as fantastic as it has been. I can feel the challenges ahead of me, but I can't let them determine my future. I love to be happy—who doesn't? But I know it doesn't come easily. Just like a fun adventure—it doesn't happen without plotting, plotting, plotting. I thought by now I'd know it all, but have learned that life doesn't change in so many ways. Just different challenges and new unchartered territories. I've learned a lot over the past few years. Most importantly, happiness doesn't just happen. Pushing myself out of my comfort zone has been my friend.

My life has been a patchwork of sorrow and happiness woven into one quilt, just like everyone else's. Some will never have the extent of pain I've had, some way more. It's all relative to each individual, and how we move forward in life can be a beautiful, constant work in progress. We have to want it. It doesn't come easily, but I've found it to be well worth it.

I look back at my pain and compare it to childbirth. I know it hurt, but that pales in comparison to the best part—my beautiful little babies. That's how I look back on the challenges of my life. I know there were tough times, and I've shared many of them; but my memories have an incredible amount of happiness, even during those times in my sea of sorrows.

It's so easy to fall back into a Bermuda Triangle of old memories, but I'm determined to make new ones. I hope that years from now, today will be a good memory also. A memory of how I didn't give up and the joy it brought to me. I don't want to be someone whose life and conversation stopped in a moment of grief that confines me to the past. My life's never going to stop. I want to build upon my life and keep exploring new territory. Of course I'll continue to tell some of those old stories. Stories that I love and that make up my history. I might even put a little color into them, too, since I'll be listening to myself telling them over and over—might as well enjoy them.

I'm meeting more and more women and men who are now experiencing the same kind of life challenges as I am. Some widowed, some divorced. The common cord between us is being alone. Recently a friend asked, "How come you get invited to couples dinners? I never do."

"When was the last time you initiated an invitation to a couple?" I asked.

"Never," she said. "I just assume they will know how lonely I am and invite me."

Well, forget it. In a social life, if one is single or married, it's a two-way street and takes some work to be included. I don't think people forget you on purpose, but if you're not on their radar screen, you won't be thought of. "Remember all the time you spent with parents of your children's friends when your children were in school, just to barely if ever see them again once your family was grown?" I asked her. If a single person, whether man or woman, wants to stay involved, they have to initiate and reach out to friendships. You just have to make yourself do it. It would be lovely if staying connected and involved were always a 50/50 effort, but you have to go the extra mile sometimes and make your effort 60/40. At other times, your friends will have to do the same for you.

It's hard—believe me—and I do feel forgotten, and many times my feelings are hurt. It's lonely. I'm not crazy about picking up the phone and saying, "Susie, do you and Jim want to go to a movie tonight?" It's weird and never becomes completely comfortable, but it does become easier, and opening myself to others is the best solution I've found to being remembered.

Just as I entertained before and during the time Don was ill, I'm now continuing on. I invite friends to my home for dinner. The table seating is now an odd number, but that's OK. I'd rather have it uneven than lose the time with friends, and they in turn then remember to include me in some of the things they're doing. It's not perfect, but it's a start.

I wrestled with the idea of going back to St. Tropez. Some local friends of mine and Don's, the Aubrys, invited me to stay with them, and after much contemplation I decided, "Hey, it's my town, too. Why should I lose it?" It was a huge challenge for me to return to a place so laden with memories of my husband and my brother. My first visit was in 1976 with my brother Don. Soon after my mother, father and other brother died, my brother Don called me and said, "What are you doing?"

"I'm planting tulips," I said from my home in Springfield, Missouri.

"Who's going to take care of them while you are in St. Tropez?" We were both recovering from a few years of family devastation, and he thought it would be fun to do something completely unexpected. I had never been to Europe and had no idea what he meant by St. Tropez.

Years later, when it became a favorite summer destination for me and my husband, he said, "Kathi, I want to meet local people. We can easily see friends passing through from the US on vacation, but I want us to become part of the local fabric of St. Tropez."

I recalled these memories as I sat at lunch at Le Club 55 with my "local friends" Judith and Alain Aubry, who embraced Don and me in a way you'd think the French never would.

I woke up each morning remembering the regiment of, "Kathi, hurry up. We need to get to town." With Don, I barely had enough time to comb my hair before we were off for a full day of lovely beaches, food, and dinner parties. It was our normal routine, but I sometimes had a hard time keeping up with it. There was absolutely no downtime during our St. Tropez visits, and now that I look back, I understand. Don was on a mission to live every second to the fullest, and boy, he did—sometimes at my expense.

Don was always on the go. The Aubrys take time to enjoy the day, a new and completely different experience. The days remind me of the ones I had as a child. Those summer days that seemed to never end.

People mistakenly feel that things in life come easily to me, but that couldn't be further from the truth. I push myself, and it isn't easy. Going to St. Tropez alone was a difficult journey to undertake. I was full of doubt and questions that I didn't have anyone to answer. What will I do with people I barely know? How will I be in the social town of Southern France by myself? How will I move to a hotel by myself? How will I stop wanting to call Don and tell him what's going on?

I finally said, "Kathi, just do it." It doesn't matter if it's a spot in Europe or being alone at the neighborhood family picnic. It's an intimidating situation, but what I'm finding out is that no one is looking at me. I can try anything, and everyone else is focused on their own life. I'm only a passing thought.

I find that being on a plane allows me the opportunity to make my own little nest where no one bothers me. It gives me some of the quietest and most private moments, like being in a cocoon or a womb. It is almost the feeling of being in a trance. When I look out the window, my mind travels effortlessly in so many directions with so many emotions.

When Don was still alive and I took a flight somewhere, it was the only time I escaped reality. I was up in the clouds, 40,000 feet above my problems. Time and solitude were my friends. I had the chance to rest without guilt and the time to write without interruptions. Emails, texts, and phone calls were all in the distance. Thousands of miles away. As I would sit and look out the window, I'd think about all sorts of things—my challenges with Don, the old life I missed with him, and often I'd jot down stories of my experiences to read to him later. He loved it when I read to him, and it didn't matter the subject. He just enjoyed the time spent together and the sound of my voice.

Even today, I feel the same way. I used to think about my past, but now I find myself thinking more about the day at hand and beyond. No matter how hard I try, it's nearly impossible for me to be uninterrupted. Just when I think I will have a few days of privacy, something comes up to throw that idea out the window. Part of it (OK, most of it) is my fault. I say yes to everything—especially when one of my children call.

"Mom, Lily's sick. Can you pick up Liam from school?"

"Mom, do you want to have lunch?" How could I possibly turn down an invitation from one of my children?

"Mom, my kids are driving me crazy. What do you think I should do?"

The list goes on and on. Before I know it, half the day is gone, and the things I needed to do for myself—writing, work, my foundation—have been squeezed out. So the peace and quiet that accompany the closing of the main cabin door also accompany my most creative hours.

Many years ago, I asked Don, "How do you do so much, running a complicated company, and never seeming stressed? How do you get so much done? You have a lot more going on than I do, and I feel overwhelmed."

"Kathi," he replied, "you need to look at the big picture and know it's out there. But only focus on a few days out." Those words have helped me ever since. I don't look too far back, too far in the future, but just wake up and do my day. When I look at life that way, it's so much easier for me to accomplish my goals, and goals are so very important to me. I don't even mean something grandiose. I try to look at life in a series of baby steps. I mean things like I need to jot down four names and make sure I ask those people to do something with me in the next couple of weeks; I need to exercise three times this week; I need to clean out my bottom drawer. It doesn't really matter what it is, but for me, having different goals on my calendar to focus on has given me a structure that helps me get through my day since I lost my Dons. It's one of the tools I used while he was ill to help get through my challenges, and it's just as effective today.

I've always kept lists and been very goal-oriented. It's part of my personality. Something Don and I had in common. Knowing that we were happiest when we had something on the horizon, I always made sure Don had something special to look forward to. It was just a new incarnation of how we'd always lived our life together.

I read somewhere that the happiest people are the ones who push themselves. I'm not sure how happy I am, but I do understand that statement. An accomplishment that is realized gives me a pride and a feeling that is mine and only mine. Something I've done. It's funny, but when I was young, I never thought I'd look at life this way, but now I see how similar every age is. It's just a matter of how one wants to play the game.

As I sat at Le Club 55 with my French friends and a renewed look on life, I saw people who were comfortable yet surprised to see me back. Within seconds, I belonged. I forced myself to go, and I am so glad I did.

I do know I'm stronger now, and I do know I'm able to live without constant sadness. I didn't think it would be possible, but I'm succeeding. It doesn't mean I don't have waves of sadness from time to time or memories that pierce my heart. What it does mean is that I am ready to embrace life again. I've turned the corner and the world is looking like a wonderful adventure again. Life didn't end with Don. For me it began. I'm now taking the love and confidence he gave me and moving forward as I know he would want me to. There's a big world out there with a lot of life to live, and I'm determined to live it.

15

BEATLES TO BOCELLI BY WAY OF MALAYSIA

"You gotta be somewhere."
—Don Koll

Last night while I was enjoying an incredible concert by Andrea Bocelli, one of The Three Tenors along with Luciano Pavarotti and Plácido Domingo, at the Hollywood Bowl, I couldn't help but think of the first time I ever went to a concert there. It's hard to believe, but it was over fifty years ago to see The Beatles. Those were the innocent days, back when going to a concert was as easy as going to the movies. When my mom was about to drop me and my girlfriends off in front of The Bowl, she thought better than to leave eight giggly teenyboppers on their own and walked right through the gate with us, even though she didn't have a ticket. Who would dare question a mother in those days? Good call, since a few years later, when I was nineteen, George Harrison asked me on a date—while I was married and pregnant.

Bocelli's music filled my heart with the memory of his voice giving life to *Le Patio*. Don played his music every afternoon over and over and over again as we sat on the veranda together watching the boats come back from a day moored off the beaches of Southern

France. Each wake bigger than the next, racing back to port as the sun was setting.

As memories of Bocelli and The Three Tenors drifted through my mind, they settled on the weekend Don and I spent in Malaysia following an annual trip to London.

Don and Kathi in Malaysia

Each June, Don and I met up with a group of friends in London for The Prince of Wales Foundation's summer events, an organization started by Prince Charles to benefit various charities he supported around the world. After the first summer of numerous parties and black-tie events, I didn't think Don would ever want to go again, but he really looked forward to it, and the sojourn became a yearly ritual. We called it our adult summer camp. We made amazing friendships with people we wouldn't normally have come across in our everyday social circle in Newport Beach. Joan Rivers kept Don in stitches with her hilarious and irreverent stories. Once, she leaned over to Don and said, "Don, look at all the fancy ladies in this room. Can you spot first, second, or third wives? Just look at their fingers. It's the size of their ring." Over the summers, we connected with many socialites, philanthropists, and other interesting people, and our adult summer camp became a ritual we all looked forward to each June.

One afternoon, we were all together in the country outside of London, along with some other groups, to watch Prince Charles playing in a polo match. There was a large tent set up where a formal luncheon was about to be served, and I noticed that Don's and my place cards were at different tables. Normally he hated that, but this time he was seated with friends whom he enjoyed. I, on the other hand, was placed at a table of people I didn't know and was worried they wouldn't speak English. As luck would have it, not only could everyone speak English but they also couldn't have been more interesting or charming. I noticed Don looking over towards me all throughout lunch. I wasn't sure if he pitied me or was envious of me.

"I am Francis Yeoh of Malaysia," the gentleman on my right introduced himself. After I introduced myself, we engaged in simple conversation until he asked, "What business is your husband in?"

"Real estate development," I answered, giving a broad description of some of Don's projects. "What about yourself?"

"I do the same thing your husband does," he said. "Plus, I own the water of England."

"The water of England? Do you mean a company like Perrier?" I asked.

"No," he said. "The utilities company."

"Oh my," I said. I wasn't sure how to respond to that one.

Mr. Yeoh and I had a wonderful conversation, and towards the end of lunch he said, "I'm having a small party on an island I own in Malaysia in honor of world peace, and I would love for you and your husband to be my guests."

"Thank you so much for the invitation. I'll talk to Don about it." A party in Malaysia with someone we didn't know? I never thought it would be something we would want to do or that I'd remember to ask.

That night as Don and I were getting ready for dinner and talking about the day, I mentioned the invitation from Francis. "Don," I said, "you won't believe it, but the guy sitting next to me asked if we'd like to come to a party he's giving on his private island in Malaysia."

"Are you kidding me?" he asked. "Are you serious? We have to go, but only for a weekend because I have too much going on at the office to be gone long."

"What?" I was dumbfounded. "You're telling me you want to go to a party in Malaysia for the weekend?"

"Kathi, I understand that part of the world from my business connections and believe me, this will be a weekend you will treasure forever. Do you think he's serious?"

"But Don, how can we fly all the way to Malaysia for a weekend? We'll be too tired." I knew what Don's response would be; I had heard it so many times before.

"Why will you be tired? Will you be digging ditches all day?" Don gave his familiar speech. "You'll be sitting on a plane and can sleep."

I found Francis that evening at the dinner we were mutually attending and accepted his kind invitation. By the time we were back home in California, a full itinerary was in our mailbox.

Within weeks we took off for Malaysia, and after over eighteen hours, the airplane touched down into Kuala Lumpur. As we exited the aircraft, there was a gentleman standing right outside the door of the plane waiting for our arrival. He quickly whisked us through security and escorted us to baggage, where he introduced us to our private porter. The porter proceeded to gather our luggage and asked us to follow him as he guided us to the monorail, which Mr. Yeoh owned, and stayed with us until we reached the city where we were met by his beautiful dark blue Mercedes. We were driven to the Ritz Carlton, owned by, of course, Mr. Yeoh, and escorted into the lobby where the general manager greeted us and handed Don a personal, handwritten note from Mr. Yeoh. He said he felt a night at the Ritz would help us with jet lag before meeting him on the island the following day. The bed in our room was already turned down and the sheets were embroidered with our monograms. To top it off, the monograms were on the correct sides. How did he know?

The next morning, we were delivered to a private airstrip where Mr. Yeoh's jet awaited us. After a quick flight to an undisclosed location, we were escorted to one of Mr. Yeoh's boats, which was standing by to take us to his island, Pangkor Laut. A Malaysian sultan had given him the island after its previous inhabitant, an exiled murderer, drank himself to death. Despite its colorful past, Mr. Yeoh transformed the small island into a luxury resort.

Don and I felt like we had just arrived on the set of *Fantasy Island*. At the end of the dock, Francis was waiting for us with two gorgeous azalea leis. The only thing missing was a white suit and Tattoo standing next to him saying, "The plane. The plane."

After settling into our beautiful seaside suite, we decided to do a little exploring around the resort. I spotted a small gift shop and persuaded Don to check it out with me. He hated shopping, but since we had time to kill, he was a good sport and walked in with me. As I looked at some trinkets, a woman asked if I'd help her pick out a wrap to wear that evening. She described her dress, and after eyeing the choices, I picked out a red cashmere shawl that seemed like it would go with what she had described. She bought it, quickly thanked me, said she looked forward to seeing us again that evening, and was off. I was quite nervous about what to wear since I didn't know any of the other guests and had no one to call to talk to about it. Most of the guests were from Asia and Europe. I think the only other American was Steve Forbes, who was asked to attend to share some of his patriotic visions for the United States. All we knew about the evening was what time we were being picked up and that the women were to wear long dresses and the men sport coats. I chose a long fuchsia dress embroidered with flowers of golden threads on the bodice, and Don wore a beige linen sport coat with white linen slacks.

As we were driven about fifteen minutes away to a small cove on the other side of the island, we wondered what the evening's festivities would be all about. When we arrived, the staff greeted us and recommended we take off our shoes to walk to the end of the beach where we would meet the other guests. Don and I walked hand in hand, me in my long pink dress, Don so handsome in his linen jacket, his tanned olive skin radiating in the glow of the sunset. As we walked down the beach, the warm sand felt soft beneath our feet and the cool water hitting our ankles felt fresh and invigorating. I never thought in a million years I would ever wear a black-tie dress on a beach and walk barefoot through the water. *This is what dreams are made from*, I thought. In the distance, we could see an archway of flowers that led us to a clearing of land where there were luxurious leather chairs set up in front of a stage framed by the natural backdrop of the island's dramatic rainforest. As we settled in amongst the other hundred guests, we could hear the water from the sea lapping up along the shore in a gentle melodic rhythm in the distance.

We were seated directly in front of Francis and his (now-deceased) wife, Rose Mary, a lovely and genteel woman who embraced me as if we had known one another for ages. We introduced ourselves to the people sitting on either side of us, but before we could engage in any kind of conversation, sixty-two members of the Philippine Symphony Orchestra walked onto the stage, followed by Luciano Pavarotti with a beautiful woman on his arm wearing a red shawl. The guests cheered with unquestionable excitement. Don glanced at me and gave his little shy smile that signified how proud he was that the total stranger I made friends with in the little gift shop was Cynthia Lawrence, who sang duets with Pavarotti for many years.

It seemed as if the music would never stop, and none of us wanted it to. This magical evening on a tiny island in Malaysia could have lasted forever. Don leaned over and whispered into my ear, "See? I told you this would be a night to remember." He added, as he always did, "It's the things in life you don't do that you most regret."

Afterwards, Cynthia and I stayed in touch. One afternoon the phone rang, and she was on the other end saying, "Kathi, I'm singing with Luciano tonight at the Staples Center in Los Angeles. Are you and Don coming?" I had no idea and hadn't bought tickets. She insisted it was no problem and offered us Pavarotti's tickets. I called Don at the office, and he was in. Of course he was—"It's the things in life you don't do that you most regret."

Our seats were front and center, and much to our surprise, we received a note that read, "Kathi and Don, please join me backstage after the performance. Luciano would love to say hi to his new friends from Malaysia."

We scampered through the crowds after their incredible performance to the stage door. We weren't sure how we'd get through all the security, but our name was on a list, and we were quickly escorted through a throng of fans waiting for a glimpse of Pavarotti.

Cynthia met us in the hallway with a huge hug. "Follow me," she said. "Luciano wants to say hi." We walked into a sizable dressing room where he sat on a large chair, his aides on either side.

"Luciano," Cynthia said, "the Kolls are here." We felt so special that he remembered us. We chatted as the others looked on with bewildered expressions. When he was awarded a Kennedy Center Honor, they described Pavarotti's early life. As a young man, he sold insurance.

After polite conversation and compliments of the evening, I said, "Mr. Pavarotti, I seem to remember that before you were an opera star, you sold insurance. What kind of insurance did you sell?"

"You sold insurance?" his aides asked in shock.

"So I sold insurance," he said in an almost Brooklyn accent with exaggerated hand movements. "What's it to ya?"

Sitting in the audience of The Hollywood Bowl, listening to the voice of Bocelli, my heart burst with these memories. *We did it*, I thought with a smile. *We won't regret anything because we embraced life and all it had to offer.* Don's mantra about regretting what you don't do never applied to us. We did it all, before and after Don's stroke.

I used to ask Don different questions and then pack his answers away. I was so surprised recently to find one, *"Are you glad you lived? I'm glad I lived to be with you,"* written on it. What a gift to see five years later.

As I've moved forward, it's been very important for me to find a purpose in my life unique to me. I love that I lived to be with Don, but I needed to find a way in which I felt I was making a difference in other people's lives. I wasn't sure what it would be, but a light bulb went off in my head one day while I was in the audience listening to a medical lecture given by Senator Bill Frist. Bill had been a close friend of ours and during the years of Don's illness had been an especially good ear to my challenges with Don. Not only was he a doctor, but his father had died on account of a stroke, so he understood the life Don and I were leading.

Bill invited me to attend a local medical conference he was speaking at on palliative care. He thought I might be interested in what his lecture was about, since I had spent so many years wrapped up in Don's medical world and had performed my own personal palliative care for him. I hadn't seen Bill since Don had passed away, and he wanted to catch up and see how I was doing.

After his speech, he found me in the audience to say hi. At the same time, a group of eager medical participants approached to meet him. One woman asked me how I knew the senator, so I shared the story of Bill's friendship, showing her pictures of Don while telling our story. "I love your passion and enthusiasm for the life you led with your husband." She showed genuine interest beyond the compassion of a stranger. "I run a division for Blue Cross in Hawaii and wonder if you'd consider speaking to a group of caregivers about how you managed the care for your husband and at the same time made a life for yourself." A few people overheard our conversation, and before I knew it, I was surrounded by a very empathetic group of people whom I had never met, asking me a million questions about my experience as a caregiver. Bill was listening intently and asked if I'd like to join him for a cup of coffee. Before the coffee was served, he said, "Kathi, you just found the purpose you've been looking for."

"What do you mean?" I asked.

"Remember when I called you not long after Don passed away, and you mentioned how you were struggling to find some kind of purpose in your life? Well, you just found it," he answered with the enthusiasm he always showed towards Don and me. "You would be a wonderful motivational speaker to caregivers. Start small, go to church groups, college classes, and community organizations to get your feet wet."

My head was swirling with thoughts, ideas, and questions.

Soon afterward, I was invited to be a member of the neurological board at Hoag Hospital in Newport Beach, and at my first meeting there was a young girl named Michelle Wulfestieg who was speaking about the tragic circumstances of a stroke she suffered at age eleven and another at age twenty-four that left her partially paralyzed. Her story was riveting, and the enthusiasm she displayed about how she lived her life with a disability was inspiring. As luck would have it, she was seated next to me.

She glanced towards my place card with my name on it and questioned, "Are you Kathi Koll? Were you married to Don Koll?"

"Yes," I answered, surprised she had any idea who I was.

"I've always wanted to meet you. I've heard of you for years and how well you cared for your husband. I actually almost knocked on your door one day."

"I so wish you would have. My husband would have loved you," I answered. "How about we meet for dinner next week?"

A week later Michelle joined me at my favorite local restaurant, Sapori a regular haunt for me and Don both before and after his stroke. We quickly got into the trials and tribulations of our life's challenges. I could see her wisdom, but could also detect the youth of a woman twenty years my junior. She shared some very personal stories that I could understand and give advice about, having the experience of one who had many more years under my belt. She had a zest for living as normally as possible, and if one hadn't watched her walk into the restaurant wearing a brace on her leg to help her walk or see her motionless arm resting on her lap, one would never notice her disability.

We connected that night, and as we walked out of the restaurant, wiping our eyes of emotion-filled tears, there was an enlightenment we had found of kindred spirits. We decided to take our show on the road. For the next eighteen months we spoke to over 1,500 people on the positive and trying aspects of "living on both sides of the hospital bed," as we titled it. I spoke as a caregiver and Michelle spoke as a patient. Together we hit on stroke, caregiving, palliative care, and hospice. Hospice being Michelle's passion. Unfortunately, I was naive about palliative care and hospice when Don was ill, so I didn't have the opportunity to experience either, but did so for Don in my own private way.

Michelle's and my first engagement was at a Rotary Club where we addressed a crowd of Rotarians before their Halloween party. I was talking to Big Bird, a saloon girl, a nun, and a bevy of others decked out in costume. The second engagement was at a senior living facility. As I presented my story about the life I led with Don, a beautiful young girl in the audience cried.

"I'm so sorry I made you cry, too," she said to me afterward. "I lost my husband a year ago and haven't had the time to grieve properly. I have two young sons, my husband had no insurance, and I'm trying to pay my bills with the first job I've ever had. Is there any chance you'd have lunch with me?"

"Of course, I'd be flattered," I answered.

We met a few weeks later and shared our stories. I'm not sure what she learned from me, but being a sounding board with no agenda seemed to make a difference. I'm happy to report that her life has taken a new twist. She met a wonderful man who embraced her young children and they married.

The audience found our stories quite emotional, and it wasn't unusual to see people wiping away their tears as we spoke, which brought tears to our own eyes many times. We were sharing personal details and connecting with the frustrations and sadness some people in the audience were experiencing. Our stories were bringing countless emotions home to them—especially those who had ill loved ones or were caring for someone. Our inspirational success was that we had both walked in very challenging shoes but weren't embarrassed to share our personal trials and tribulations to help show how one can have a successful and enriched life even under many difficult circumstances.

After almost two years we moved on, evolving in separate directions. Michelle was starting a family, and between her hospice job and new role as a mother, our time constraints were different.

Working with Michelle helped me discover the passion I wanted to focus on, the one I have the most experience with, being a caregiver. Those eighteen months were a lesson in what worked for me and how I could best help others in my own quest for purpose.

I started Kathi's Caregivers under the umbrella of The Kathi Koll Foundation to emphasize the role of family caregivers in need, and when I say in need, I mean those who can't afford any kind of respite. I understand the loneliness, the sadness, the frustrations, the depression, the helplessness, the guilt. The difference is that I could afford to take time for myself. Not that I did enough of it, but at least I didn't have the additional stress gnawing at me of how I could afford for my loved one and myself to survive.

One of my favorite TV shows as a child was *The Millionaire*. Raymond Burr would show up at an unsuspecting home and give away a million dollars. I loved watching the emotionally packed surprise and hearing the stories of why they were chosen. In that same spirit, Don and I used to pick unsuspecting young couples at restaurants and secretly pay for their dinner. It was really fun to watch them look all over the room and try to guess who had just given them such a surprising gift.

In my own way, that's what I'm doing now. It's not a million dollars, but to the recipient, it feels like it. My gifts are small, meaningful help to give a bit of respite not only financially, but most important, emotionally. Some of these people are so alone, so scared, so incredibly sad. I hear their stories, and after being vetted by a clinic or recommended in various ways, the caregiver and I meet, and I let them know they aren't alone; and I offer some financial support to help alleviate a specific problem unique to them. All of this is done through the very generous support of family, friends, and community to help me in this quest. The fact that a complete stranger appears to help them is an emotional bonus that resonates deeply.

I've also found wonderful satisfaction in writing blogs that stem from what I learned during my experiences as a caregiver. I've found myself saying, "I wished I had known me when the catastrophic, life-turning events happened to me and Don." It gives me an opportunity to help the caregivers I can reach out to personally and financially. Giving tips that worked for me. Sharing feelings I had. Offering ideas I've tried. The funny thing is that I find myself rereading them. A few reminders go a long way in keeping me on a positive track. Sometime I'll read one and think, *I'm not perfect, for Christ's sake.* But the reminder to look up always helps.

AFTERWORD

"I am the master of my fate,
I am the captain of my soul."
—William Ernest Henley

One morning as I was sipping my coffee and breezing through my mail I spotted what looked to be something special from the Abbey of Regina Laudis. I quickly opened it to find a beautiful invitation to attend the 50th Year Jubilee Celebration for Mother Dolores, commemorating her five-decade role in the community of the Abbey of Regina Laudis. It cam as an utter surprise having not realized that so many years had passed. I wanted to go, but the effort felt daunting. My kids and their families were all busy making their own memories and traditions. I would be flying alone across the country, changing planes, renting a car, and driving through rural Connecticut. Of course I wanted to, but a part of me that couldn't be ignored didn't want to go. I kept wondering, *Is this for me, Mother Dolores, or for my brother?* So I had tucked the invitation away under a pile of to-do tasks on my desk.

As the time approached, and I was assured of a solo weekend at home, I thought, *What the heck—ya gotta be somewhere.* I quickly emailed Mother Dolores that I was coming, and by her response I knew I was doing the right thing. She was genuinely excited; she even called numerous times after her email. This wasn't a connection to my brother; it was our newfound personal friendship. After my Dons died, we became friends on our terms, and I was glad I wasn't going for anyone else. This was for me. I was heading out with a new feeling of optimism. I felt a different emotional make up than I'd felt on the trip a few years earlier. How times had changed. I was now becoming my own person, freeing myself of the everyday grief that had haunted me for so long. Life was now on my terms.

Once again, I found myself driving through the rolling hills of Connecticut. Each turn brought memories of my brother, which in turn engaged thoughts of my husband. This had been the journey I made a few years ago when I was looking for something I couldn't quite grasp to help soothe my sorrow, help me resolve thoughts to unanswered questions, and help me understand why my life had taken so many cruel turns.

Just as before, the little white-framed guesthouse was nestled along the side of the road, but this time the pond was dry. Had there been an unusually dry summer? The sign announcing the Abbey of Regina Laudis greeted me like a familiar friend. This time, though, I knew to take a different turn. Not towards the Abbey but up a narrow, tree-lined road toward the chapel where Mass would begin the weekend celebration promptly at 10:00 AM.

* * *

"Mother Dolores is so excited you're here," Mother Angele whispered enthusiastically in my ear as she hugged me. I liked her electric personality from the minute I met her years earlier when she accompanied Mother Dolores the day she visited my husband in Beverly Hills. I was always so intrigued by her life and the path that led her to the abbey. She had been an agent for opera singers for thirty years, converted to Catholicism from Judaism, and to put the cherry on top, she was my brother's goddaughter.

She escorted me to a reserved spot in the front row. My first thought was to sit in the seat my brother always chose, but I thought, *I'm me. I'm making my own new memories, and I'm not here for anyone or any reason other than the fact I want to be.* I had made the journey to help celebrate fifty years of devotion to God by a former actress, former fiancée, kinda sister-in-law, and former prioress—the celebration of the journey Mother Dolores Hart had chosen. Walking past a full congregation of three hundred friends and family made me feel pretty special to be a part of that journey.

I sat quietly waiting for the ceremony to begin. The altar stretched out in front of me but stayed separated by the monastic iron grille. I felt an air of excitement filling the chapel as people chatted and discovered the ties that bound them to Mother Dolores. The lady next to me had been a friend of Mother Dolores since the seventh grade, and her family had made the trip from South Carolina. Maria Cooper Janus was checking out the microphone, which led me to believe she was going to share a few words. The gentleman behind me was fascinating. He shared his story of how Mother Dolores' movie *Lisa*—about a woman who had survived the Holocaust—had made such an impact on him as a young man that he almost converted to Judaism. He had contacted Mother Dolores only in recent years through letters, but her counseling and friendship had helped him through some life-altering problems. He and his wife were now regulars at the Abbey and excited to cheer on Mother Dolores for her monumental day.

The side door opened quietly, and one by one the community of nuns walked in, single file, hands clasped in prayer, voices clear and as beautiful as nightingales singing from the heavens above. I spotted Mother Dolores as she glanced my way and gave me a little smile radiating with the unspoken message, "I'm so happy you're here."

That evening I sat down and wrote a letter to my family:

Dear family,

I'm so glad I came to Mother Dolores' 50ᵗʰ Jubilee, and I think all of you would have found it meaningful too. It's hard to put the experience into words, but what I do want to share is the love the community had for Uncle Don. Not just the sisters but so many people I met. There was a part of his life I never knew to such an extent.

I know you all loved Uncle Don, but being here has shown me a far deeper and private side he didn't share with us. He used to say he was shy, but now I am closer to understanding what he meant by that. It wasn't so much shyness in the typical sense. No, it was shyness in not bragging about what he did for so many people and what he meant to them.

Kathi's brother Don

As mother Dolores said to Don my husband, "Love doesn't always end at the altar." It has been beautiful to feel and witness a different kind of love. Not just from Dolores but from this entire community of Regina Laudis. They cherished him, and he made a difference in their lives.

For the first time, I learned how far his love and unselfishness went. Countless guests from all walks of life, from so many places, shared what Uncle Don meant to them. Apparently he spent time talking with many of them, whether on the phone or when visiting the Abbey. His wisdom had far-reaching tentacles. Story after story, "You're Don's sister? He was there for me when I needed help, when I needed advice, for when I was in despair."

Constantly learning is an adventure no matter what it is. Learning this other side, or at least a more detailed side, of the love Uncle Don gave to so many has been a gift. We were all truly blessed to have had him in our lives.

Love,
Mom

Kathi and Mother Dolores

It's one of life's "you had to be there" moments. I know only that it was right for me, and I'm so happy I made the "daunting" journey. Yes, I thought of my brother; I thought of my husband. I also thought of how the circle of life can be a beautiful thing along with all of its unbearable challenges. It's getting through those challenges that has given me strength. Of course I didn't like them at the time, but I do relish in the fact that through those times I have grown, learned, cried, laughed, loved, and above all else realized I can handle what life sends my way, and survive. There will be more, I'm sure. I'm bracing myself.

"I am a Kick-Ass Kinda Girl." ☺

ABOUT THE KATHI KOLL FOUNDATION

I wrote *Kick-Ass Kinda Girl* as a way to share my story with others on this journey, and to remind them they're not walking alone. No two experiences are the same, but the loss of love and self, and the fear and sadness, are shared by all of us. It's my prayerful hope that fellow caregivers who read this book will know they are not alone.

The Kathi Koll Foundation was created in 2014 to provide meaningful support to caregivers in need. The foundation offers short-term financial subsidies for struggling caregivers and a community education program geared toward helping people navigate the various challenges that can arise. Kathi's Caregivers, a branch of the foundation, helps caregivers whose lives are dedicated to their loved ones to know they aren't alone while juggling their caregiving and personal responsibilities. The foundation's goal is to help improve the lives of caregivers and their families. More information can be found at www.KathiKollFoundation.org.

ABOUT THE AUTHOR

Kathi and her family reside in Southern California. She is the mother of three children and the extremely proud grandmother of nine grandchildren, who lovingly call her KK. When she isn't helping and educating caregivers, she is traveling all over the world, looking for new adventures.

To view more pictures from Kathi Koll's album please visit KathiKoll.com

ACKNOWLEDGMENTS

I can't begin to thank or remember all the people who have helped me on this journey. I raise my glass and thank you all for your friendship and encouragement through all my adventures.

This book captures the spirit of my experience to the best of my recollection. Others may remember or interpret certain events and conversations differently. I don't pretend to remember every exchange verbatim, but I've done my best to remain true to the spirit of conversations and events. I do not consider myself a medical or legal expert, and no part of this manuscript should be construed or misconstrued as medical or legal information or advice.

My brother Don, who took my hand as a little girl and guided me till the day I lost him, you were one in a million, never to be replaced.

My husband, Don, you took me on a journey that taught me so much about love, tenacity, and life. You opened my cage and encouraged me to fly. Because of our life together, I have no regrets. There will forever be a corner of my heart full of our memories.

To my children, Jennifer, Kevin, and Brooke, without whom life would have little meaning. No matter the time of day, you've been there to wipe away my tears and help me smile. What a role reversal!

To the "Outlaws" Rick, Melissa, and Chris, you're not outlaws or in-laws. You're my family, and I'm so lucky each of my children found you. Together the seven of us are a force to be reckoned with.

To my nine grandchildren, Ryder, Flynn, Kathi, Donovan, Braden, Hill, Liam, Lily, and Tommy, who give me a reason to kick up my heels! Your KK loves you.

Jack, you are not just my stepson, but you and Carter are among my closest friends. Thank you for the love your dad felt from you. Especially when the going got tough.

Abby, you're with your buddy now. You never left his side, or mine after Don was gone.

To Nancy Brinker, who came up with this idea to begin with. You said I could do it. I didn't believe you.

To Joni and Jerusha Rodgers. I could never have done this without you. Thank you for your encouragement, lessons, edits, and helping me write my story, which also helped me move through rough waters and come out whole again. I love the fact I have only known you through words until recently, and how wonderfully our words represented us.

To Bonnie for always having an ear to listen with and wise advice for me to ponder.

Watty, I'm going to let you fill in the blanks. You always make me smile, and when the good times were long past, you and Kimmy—and Donna and Greg—were there with unwavering loyalty, helping DK smile again.

Mac, I will never forget the "new room, food in the fridge, and your friendship." You always make me laugh.

Nettie and Chery, my rocks. Thank you for holding me up so many times. Words can't come close to expressing my love for the two of you. I only wish every caregiver who reads this book will have two angels like you, with Ken as their leader.

Jenny, you are the perfect *National Enquirer* reader.

Phil. "Mr. Koll, if I could drive your car, carry your briefcase, anything." Don was always so proud to be your mentor.

Byron, Ron, Paul, Don had so many friends that they could fill up a book of their own, but you three shine like the North Star. Thank you for never leaving his side.

Ray, I so appreciate your friendship and loyalty then and now. You are the guardian angel DK sent to me.

To Dr. John Storch. Thank you for the many long hours and support you gave Don—especially in those first harrowing weeks.

Dr. BZ, thank you for your unabated willingness to help, and for your drive to build the Hoag Stroke Center to the impressive facility it is today.

Senator Frist, thank you for encouraging me to open up my life. Hopefully my journey will help others in times of despair to see that life can have many rainbows.

Shannon, Susie, Nancy, and Sheila, I've smiled many smiles on account of your friendship—especially your colorful performance one Cabo afternoon. DK's eyes are still...well, you know.

Team DK led by Dr. Shpiner: Thank you for helping Don have a life impossible for most. Your devotion and love for my husband was obvious. As difficult as my loss of privacy was, the DK Team was my lifeline, and I miss all of you to this day.

TQ, thank you for your continued friendship and for being one of the first people at Don's side. To think it all started with kilts.

Deborah, thanks for your idea, "Kathi, when you're sad and can't decide who to call for help, just put twenty names in a bowl, close your eyes, and pick one." It was a brilliant idea!

Bob and O'Malley, thank you for sticking with me.

Robin and Dottie, Gail, Susy, Audrey, and Libby, you were and are my cheer and support.

John and Sharon, your shoulders are huge. Thank you for giving me every inch.

GH, thank you for forty years of friendship and encouraging me to share my story. Lucky me. We now get to share another forty years.

QUESTIONS FOR DISCUSSION

1. What do you think motivated Kathi to tell her life story?

2. Chapter 1, titled "The Visual Girl," references a television show that Kathi was in as a young girl and details Kathi's life before her marriage to Don Koll. How does "The Visual Girl" describe this stage of her life?

3. How do you think the death of Kathi's mother when she was such a young woman and the illnesses that plagued her father and brothers have framed Kathi's character and caregiving nature?

4. The relationship between Mother Dolores and Kathi's brother Don reveals a devotion that surpasses the traditional view of a love affair. In fact, Mother Dolores says, "Love does not end at the altar." What does she mean by this?

5. Kathi describes the day that her husband suffered his catastrophic stroke as the dividing line between the two lives she had with him— going from the peak of the mountain to the bottom of the sea. How did Kathi's outlook on life change, or did it?

6. One of Don's doctors counseled Kathi: "Make sure Don doesn't just live to exist. Make sure he exists to live." What does this advice mean to you?

7. Don had told Kathi, "*There are only three things in life that really matter: food, water, and love. Food and water enable one to exist. Love*

enables one to live." Did Kathi and Don's love and devotion to each other help Don live longer despite the medical realities of his condition? How has your love enabled someone to live more fully?

8. Kathi realized that the best way to give Don strength, happiness, and a will to live would be to allow him to think that, despite the stroke, he was still in charge. She says, "I would be in charge but never let him know that he wasn't." How did this approach affect Don's attitude?

9. Despite Kathi's outward appearance of strength, inside she was suffering from an emotional roller coaster. If you have ever cared for someone who was sick, did you find yourself holding back true emotions while putting on a brave face? Through therapy Kathi discovered that in her efforts to make life as normal as possible for Don, she had ignored her own needs. Are there situations in your own life when this has happened to you?

10. Kathi describes the "anticipated grief" she experienced not knowing if Don would still be alive when she woke up the next day, or whether he would still be with her at the end of that day. This can be harder to endure than caring for someone with a terminal illness, because the end is unknown. How can one cope with this uncertainty?

11. What role does Mother Dolores play in Kathi's life? Does she provide more than spiritual solace and companionship?

12. The book begins and ends with Kathi visiting Mother Dolores at the Abbey. How do these visits serve to bookend Kathi's story and the lives of her two Dons?

13. Were there experiences—either positive or negative—that Kathi had or things that she did for Don or for herself that can help you or someone you know who's in a caregiving role? What were they?

14. The jacket art features a cactus and popped and floating balloons. What do you think the balloons represent? The cactus? Could they be symbolic of one's resilient nature and strength despite life's adversity or fragility? What other thoughts do you have about the jacket art?

15. How did you react to the title of Kathi's memoir? Does it reflect her gutsy nature?

16. Was there anything about Kathi's life that you wished she had written about in more detail?

17. Do you need to have been or to be a caregiver in order to appreciate Kathi's story? Or is there inspiration to be found for any reader? Would you recommend this book to a friend?

Made in the USA
San Bernardino,
CA